Unlock Your Inner Superhero:
Conquering the Challenges of ADHD

Hannah Bookbinder, LSW, M.Ed., creator of My TOAD App™
Illustrations by Annika Winkelmann

Philadelphia, PA

Printed in the United States of America
Editing: Kimberly Coghlan, Coghlan Professional Writing Services
Cover Design: Karen Captline, BetterBe Creative
Paperback ISBN: 979-8-9985231-0-6
Ebook ISBN: 979-8-9985231-0-6
Audio ISBN: 979-8-9985231-2-0

Praise for
Unlock Your Inner Superhero

"If you have ADHD or love someone who does, this book is a must-read. Hannah Bookbinder's work validated and articulated lifelong struggles I've fought to understand. Her book helped explain a lot of daily struggles I have that I hadn't attributed to ADHD and hadn't been able to clearly identify until now.

"This book perfectly captures the unique challenges and strengths of the ADHD mind in a way that makes readers feel truly seen. It provides not only a deeper understanding and acceptance of the condition but also actionable, effective strategies to support and manage your 'superpower'."

Anna Mallory, client and student living with ADHD

"This book is a must-read for all young people struggling with ADHD, as well as for the caring adults (parents, teachers, and behavioral health providers) who play important roles in their lives. Written in a conversational and positive manner, this book not only covers the usual core symptoms of ADHD and strategies to overcome them, but importantly also gives valuable insight into the way that a client's ADHD can affect their lives in indirect but important ways. Chapters on topics such as family dynamics, social media, and others are rarely included in books on ADHD and yet can be some of the most impactful issues affecting the ADHD client. I plan to use this book as a resource for working with my clients on a daily basis!"

Craig Coleman, M.D., Assistant Professor of Psychiatry at the University of Pittsburgh School of Medicine and Attending Child and Adolescent Psychiatrist, UPMC

"What an amazing tool for ADHD students. This book gives practical advise on how to handle schoolwork by using tools, exercises, and stop-and-reflect questions. The thoughtful writing style makes it easy to read and helps students feel comfortable with managing their ADHD."
Robin Bass, parent of child living with ADHD

"Finally, a practical book designed for young people grappling with executive functioning challenges! Hannah Bookbinder clearly knows these teenagers who are overwhelmed by ADHD, anxiety, and a range of learning and organizational difficulties. In **Unlock Your Inner Superhero: Conquering Challenges of ADHD** she provides readers with strategies for navigating school, work, and the minefield of life. Each chapter provides validation, knowledge, and specific techniques that are easy to understand. This is a "must read" for parents and teachers at a time when an increasing number of young people feel overwhelmed and stressed. I highly recommend it to teachers, counselors, parents and their teens or young adults who will read the real-life examples and think: 'That's me! I am not alone.'"
Penny Moldofsky, Director of the Center for Literacy and Learning at Woodlynde School

"This book is delightful and will be a helpful tool for people with ADHD. The vignettes are relatable and topical. The exercises are very beneficial. This is a must read!!"
Janet Snellenburg-Kline, MSS, LCSW, Coordinator of Student Services at a suburban Philadelphia private school

"Perfect playbook for ADHD patients, parents, educators, physicians, and psychologist. Manual does not "tell you about ADHD and how to fix it," but speaks ADHD jargon that every patient has experienced (from social to academic) and carefully takes readers step-by-step to fully comprehend that the power lies within. While navigating and participating in the process, they can begin to identify and implement the strategies needed to be successful without medication.

This book is a major first step that doesn't take weeks of sessions and money to get their jumping off point. It's an entire re-organization and rethinking of how the ADHD brain works, and then redirecting it for success, socially, academically, and professionally.

"I wish I had this 40 years ago when we had little information, a few educators, and one drug lasting three hours that the patient needed to take multiple times a day (every 3 hours) to get through the day, and there were many side effects. This would frustrate patients, parents and educators.

"Today, at the first meeting with patients and families, we would give them this workbook for all members to read and help implement with their physicians, educators, and therapists. Together, this care team should be able to follow a roadmap for success. This valuable tool allows full comprehension of ADHD challenges and offers a solid work solution."

Maddy Weiser, pediatrician, suburban Philadelphia

Dedication

To Bu Bu, Evan, and Zach. You inspire me every day to be the best wife, mom, and person I can be. I love you to the moon, the stars, beyond, and back.

Table of Contents

Introduction i

    Formatting And Presentation iv

    Validation.. iv

    Knowledge v

    Strategies v

    Examples.. vii

Chapter 1 Unmasking Your Superpowers: Understanding ADHD and Other Challenges 1

    What Is ADHD? 3

    How Common Is ADHD? 4

    How Is ADHD Diagnosed? 5

    I Heard There Are Different Types Of ADHD. Is This True? 5

    How Does ADHD Impact a Person's Life?.............................. 6

    The News is Not All Bad:.. 9

    Is There Anything Else I Need to Know? 11

    Dishonesty 12

Chapter 2 The Anxious Hero: Conquering Anxiety and Achieving Academic Excellence 17

    Can You Relate? 18

    Strategies 21

    Deep Breathing 32

    Mindfulness Exercises... 33

    Separation of Work and Play 34

    Stress-Relieving Activities 35

Chapter 3 The Truth, the Lie, and the Unfinished Homework: ADHD's Tangled Web of Deception 47

    What's Really Going On? 48

    Good Enough Is Enough 64

    Real-Life Example... 68

Chapter 4 Perfectly Imperfect: Embracing Imperfections to Reach Academic Success..**73**

Impact...75

Triggers 76

Strategies...80

Utilize Your Academic Strategies 82

Unpack Your Fear...82

Recognize Your Own Strengths.....................................83

Conclusion 88

Chapter 5 Stand Tall and Speak Loud: The Art of Self-Championing 91

Calming the Frustration 92

Self-Advocacy 93

Why Do Kids with ADHD Struggle to Ask for Help? 95

Why Asking for Help is Critical to Your Success 99

Strategies...102

Build Your Self-Confidence 108

Recognize Your Own Strengths....................................109

Look at Your Track Record..110

Be Realistic with Your Expectations 110

Chapter 6 The Parent-Student Dynamic Duo: Trust, Triumph, and Lots of Patience!...**115**

Managing Relationships 116

So, How Do We Stop the Madness? 122

Strategies...131

Chapter 7 From FOMO to Focus: Finding Balance in the Social Media Sphere **137**

Managing Social Media 138

General Guidelines for Family 154

Suggestion for Time Blindness.....................................155

Suggestions for Boredom 156

Suggestions for Social Interaction................................156

Practice In-Person Interactions....................................158

Engage in Activities that Require Patience: 158

Conclusion: Let's Bring It Home................................**165**

    Finding Resilience 166

    Closing Thoughts 173

Assume a Superhero Pose...**175**

Take Action!..**177**

    Apps.. 190

    Books 190

    Magazine 192

    Websites 192

    YouTube 192

    Organizer 193

Introduction

If you're reading this book, you may be interested in learning more about Attention-Deficit Hyperactivity Disorder (ADHD) and the challenges that often accompany this neurodevelopmental disorder. Perhaps you have ADHD, and maybe a parent, guardian, or caretaker gave you this book—or even *forced* you to read it. If that's the case, you may feel frustrated, overwhelmed, or even annoyed because your ADHD already feels like a major roadblock in your life, kicking you in the rear daily. I get it. The last thing you want to do is to read a book about the very thing that makes you miserable.

Sorry for my bluntness. Since parents may read this, I have to be somewhat appropriate—or do I? I believe in the importance of honesty. As I tell all my clients, my best help is based on *their* best information. So, there's no need to dress it up. It's better to tell it like it is.

So, who am I, and what makes me an *expert* on ADHD? I'm Hannah Bookbinder, LSW, M.Ed., an academic coach and owner of AcademicAlly, LLC, a boutique practice serving students who face challenges in school—and in many other facets of life.

For over twenty-five years, I've worked with thousands of students who struggle with time management, organization, self-advocacy, accountability, focus, and study skills. I understand the frustration, shame, anxiety, and exhaustion that often accompany neurodivergence. My experience in this field has given me a deep understanding of the nuances of ADHD, allowing me to develop tried-and-true strategies tailored to the unique learning profile of each of my students.

I'm going to take a wild guess about what led you to these pages. If you're a student, maybe your teachers and parents are constantly on your case. Your grades aren't where they should be, and assignments are late or missing. In class, you're fourteen minutes into a daydream when your teacher calls on you, publicly humiliating you with a question you didn't even hear. You're left sputtering, trying to formulate a response that sounds remotely intelligent to save face in front of your smirking peers.

Each night, you spend hours trying to *start* your homework, let alone finish it. The mere thought of tackling this undesirable task feels overwhelming—like a life sentence in prison. No matter how much effort or time you put in, it's never enough to get the job done well, and the payoff seems hardly worth it. Then, the fights with the adults in your life begin, which could be perfect fodder for a nightly newscast: "Extra, extra! World War III is about to begin!" The situation is hopeless. Life sucks, and you're at your breaking point.

But you're still here, and you're reading my book....

If that's you, then let me congratulate you. I know it's not easy listening to or reading this book. I understand the amount of mental energy it takes to focus while reading. And, depending on the time of year, you may feel exhausted after a full day of classes, followed by demanding extra-curricular activities. Or, it may be summer, and you're in your happy place in the mountains, at your summer camp, or at the beach—and as I said earlier, the last thing you want to do is read about the very thing that causes you so much angst.

I get it. You'll see me mention that a lot because I understand your issues, and I sympathize with you. Still, you should know you're taking one of the most important steps to help yourself. It may have been someone else's idea to read this book, but now, it's in your hands, and if you've made it this far into the introduction, then I must be saying something that resonates.

Some of you may think, "Who does this woman think she is? Why is her book important?" Look, I don't think I'm that special, but after more than twenty-five years of working with clients like you, I'm well-versed in living with ADHD and its challenges.

I've worked tirelessly to develop and refine a variety of strategies to support diverse learning profiles, and they really do work. It's not magic; you'll need to put in consistent effort to see results. And the ride won't always be smooth—you'll face frustration, and you won't always "get it." But as the pilot of your plane, you have the power to control your flight and shape the quality of your journey. I'll be here as your co-pilot... just you and me.

Now, I'd like to address parents and caregivers. While I've primarily written this book for students, I encourage you to continue reading and to experience it from your child's perspective. Living with ADHD can be challenging, and it's enlightening to put yourself in someone else's shoes. Plus, you may find that the strategies in this book will help you strengthen your relationship with your child—and decrease the endless arguments that often surround those with ADHD.

Now, let's look at the road map:

Formatting And Presentation

I understand that your attention span for this type of activity may be short, and time is even shorter. With each chapter, I'll strive to be concise and direct. The format of this book will include the following:

- Identifying and explaining challenges
- Strategies to address the challenges
- Personal anecdotes

By presenting information in this manner, you can use this book to your advantage, easily identifying and perusing the pages that apply to your experience—and skipping those that don't. I designed this book's structure to help you read deliberately, reflect on what is helpful, and consider how you might apply this information to your daily habits.

Now that we have a road map for our journey, you might wonder, "What's in it for me?" Read on, my friend!

Validation

How many times have you felt like someone really understood your experience? Have you ever sought help from someone who sympathized with your frustration, anger, or despair—someone who recognized how overwhelming it can be? Did you wish they appreciated your smallest victories, knowing that each minor triumph meant you were finally moving in the right direction? I understand this because I see it with my clients every day. I understand these challenges—and I also recognize the excitement of achieving a win.

Knowledge

By now, you're likely an expert on life with ADHD and could probably list its drawbacks with your eyes closed. But do you truly understand what ADHD is and why it wreaks havoc on your life? Are you aware of the gifts that come with this disorder?

One of the many attributes I admire about the ADHD mind is the ability to think outside the box. My clients view issues from different perspectives, considering various aspects to form plausible solutions. Watching my students troubleshoot and strategize is fascinating because they create solutions that work for themselves—*and* for the greater good. It's truly incredible. Together, we will discover your hidden superpowers!

Strategies

I will present and explain strategies to address the daily challenges you face as a student. Each strategy will include a detailed explanation, helping you understand how it works and how to apply it, both inside *and* outside of the classroom. You'll have access to specific tools and exercises to practice these strategies immediately. These techniques are typically only available to my clients—but now they're accessible to you, my readers. We'll cover the following areas:

Organizational Skills: In the world of ADHD, backpacks often resemble the scene of an explosion. Important papers get crumpled, pencils are splintered, and snacks are pulverized, while the rotting remains just might offer the cure for cancer. Whether it's your bookbag, your workspace, or your bedroom, I'll offer a variety of suggestions to help you get organized in no time.

Time Management: Time blindness often plagues individuals with ADHD. What should take thirty minutes can easily stretch into two hours due to hyper-focus or distractions. We'll explore tools and tips to help you become more aware of time and manage it effectively.

Motivation: What motivates you? Are you motivated by external factors—like positive feedback from parents, teachers, or friends? Do you love material rewards for strong performances? Or are you driven by personal pride and the desire to succeed? Let's work together to uncover your true motivation and use that information to propel you toward success.

Initiation: Sometimes, starting an assignment is the hardest part of sitting down to do homework. Is something more interesting drawing your attention? Are you overwhelmed with a specific task because it feels like it will take forever to complete? Do you find it difficult to understand what's being asked of you? By demystifying the reasons behind your immobility, we can identify strategies to help you feel more confident in tackling the task at hand.

Accountability: Whether we like it or not, knowing we will be held accountable for our choices can help us complete a task—and motivate us to do it correctly. I'll teach you some tricks to enhance your own self-accountability.

Self-advocacy: Asking for help can be difficult for many of us. It often feels uncomfortable to put ourselves in a vulnerable position. We may feel we should already know the answers, and we don't want to burden our teachers or professors. Sometimes, we may not even realize what we don't know, leaving us spinning out. This book will help you identify what's holding you back—and provide strategies to overcome those obstacles.

STOP and Think: Of the areas listed above, which ones do I struggle with the most?

_____

_____

_____

_____

_____

_____

_____

_____

_____

_____

Examples

No matter what our goals are, it's always helpful to hear stories about people who have walked the walk—they understand the trials and tribulations we have encountered. For confidentiality, the names of clients have been changed, but real people and authentic experiences matter.

Those with ADHD understand the nuances that come with this disorder, and it's not always about mind over matter. Sometimes, it's about the time of day, what's happening on social media, what meds you took, _when_ you took them, or the internal noise that makes it difficult to focus on creating a simple sentence, let alone an entire essay.

Clients I have worked with understand the frustration and lack of self-worth that often accompany ADHD. They have experienced the knock-down, drag-out battles that unfold nightly in many households where ADHD is present.

Why is it so helpful to include real-life examples of students who have walked in your shoes? First, they offer hope. Students who struggle with the challenges of ADHD and other learning profiles often wonder whether success is even possible. Reading about peers who have been there and done that provides much-needed inspiration and hope. By learning about individuals who have overcome similar obstacles and achieved their goals, you can see that it's possible to thrive and excel.

Your experienced peers can normalize your journey. Struggling with ADHD or other learning profiles can often feel isolating, as it may feel like no one understands your challenges and frustrations. By sharing stories of other students who have faced similar struggles, we can prove that you're not alone—and that others have walked the same path.

By hearing what others have experienced, you can discover practical strategies that have worked for them. After reading about their innovative methods to manage time, stay organized, or engage with their studies, you can adapt these ideas to suit your needs, your personality, and your learning style. These examples can become valuable resources, illuminating the path to success and offering practical tools to help you accomplish your goals.

The stories of those who have triumphed over adversity are inherently motivating. Witnessing how others have faced obstacles with resilience and determination can ignite a fire within you. These stories will serve as a reminder that setbacks and challenges are a natural part of life, but they *don't* have to define your future. These narratives will motivate you to keep pushing forward, even in the face of difficulties.

Finally, reading about the successes of others fosters a sense of self-efficacy—the belief in your ability to accomplish tasks and reach your goals. Real-life stories show that success is not reserved for a select few but is achievable for anyone willing to put in the effort and seek the right strategies. As you absorb these examples, you'll find your confidence growing.

Remember, the real-life examples shared in this book are not intended to offer a one-size-fits-all solution. Instead, they will serve as guides, offering insights, inspiration, and practical strategies that you can adapt to suit your own unique needs. These stories will illuminate the possibilities that lie ahead and empower you to embrace your strengths to overcome obstacles standing in your way.

On a final note, you may be wondering why I chose the toad for my book. Toads are often associated with change and evolution-they begin as slimy eggs, develop into cute, roly-poly tadpoles, and finish their development as little creatures that are so ugly, you can't help but fall in love with them! The toad also represents my executive functioning app I developed. My TOAD App™, was created for people across the lifespan who, just like you, struggle with time management, organization, accountability, and distractibility. Utilizing my clinically-proven strategies, this app offers user-friendly tools that will help you to organize your tasks and assignments, develop a sense of time, minimize your distractions, and hold you accountable. For more information, scan the QR code at the end of this chapter.

The time we are about to spend together is all about you. It's not about pleasing the adults in your life. The goal is not to ignite a passion for learning—although, if you think about it, would that really be so bad? Still, this is about working smarter, not harder. It's establishing a relationship of trust—not with me, but with yourself, so that when you reach the end of this book, you have the confidence, sense of self-efficacy, and grit to face the challenges that come with having ADHD.

Yes, you have a neurodevelopmental disorder, and you may face additional challenges from other circumstances as well. However, it's important to be proactive and to identify strategies to support yourself so these challenges won't define you.

Trust your experiences, embrace these strategies, believe in yourself, and embark on a powerful transformation toward success. Together, let's supercharge your ADHD and empower you to thrive.

Check out My TOAD App™:

STOP and Think: What are my goals for reading this book?

_____
_____
_____
_____
_____
_____
_____
_____
_____
_____
_____
_____

Chapter 1
Unmasking Your Superpowers: Understanding ADHD and Other Challenges

In this chapter, we embark on a journey to unmask the superpower within you. ADHD. Attention-Deficit/Hyperactivity Disorder (ADHD) is not a limitation but a unique cognitive wiring that brings a diverse range of learning profiles. Just as each superhero possesses distinct extraordinary abilities, individuals with ADHD showcase an array of strengths and talents.

Before we begin, let's drop into your math class. Picture this. You're sitting in a classroom, fidgeting in your seat, your mind buzzing with a million thoughts. *After school, I need to walk the dog... did I remember to clean up my room before I left for school today? Shoot! I have to remind Mom to sign that permission slip for our trip to the museum....*

It's pretty busy inside of that brain of yours. In the meantime, the teacher's droning on about quadratic equations, and let's be honest. She's *not* keeping your attention. Maintaining your attention is often like trying to catch a squirrel sprinting toward a yummy array of leftover food at a neighborhood ballpark. Meanwhile, your classmates seem to have their acts together, focused and engaged—like miniature Einsteins in the making. How do they do it?

Fear not! You, my friend, are about to discover the extraordinary capabilities that come with your neurodivergence. Think of it as having a secret stash of superpowers the rest of the world has yet to fully comprehend. Imagine if you had the superpower of hyper-focus—the ability to immerse yourself in a task or subject that truly captures your interest. It would be as if you were the Sherlock Holmes of concentration, dissecting complex problems or exploring fascinating topics with laser-like precision. You'd possess the remarkable ability to see patterns, connections, and solutions that others miss entirely.

And let's not forget about your incredible creativity. Your brain is like a fireworks display, bursting with ideas and imagination that dazzle the world around you. Not unlike the artist, Leonardo da Vinci, whose ADHD mind crafted masterpieces like the *Mona Lisa* and *The Last Supper*, your ability to see the world differently, to think outside the box, is a gift that can change lives and shape the future.

But wait, there's more! You can harness your hyperactivity into an energy source that fuels your endeavors. It's like having the tireless conviction of Usain Bolt, the fastest man on the planet. Bolt's electrifying speed and boundless energy propelled him to Olympic gold medals, and he shattered world records in the sport of sprinting. Just as Bolt transformed his hyperactivity into a superpower on the track, you, too, can channel your energy into pursuits that inspire and motivate you.

Of course, it's essential to acknowledge the challenges that come with ADHD and diverse learning profiles. The struggles with focus, time management, and organization can feel like trying to corral a herd of caffeinated cats, but we'll explore practical strategies to help you overcome these hurdles and present your superpowers to the world.

So, dear reader, as we peel back the layers to unlock the full potential of your ADHD and diverse learning profile, remember to embrace your quirks, your strengths, and your unique perspective. Together, we'll launch into a journey of exploration and dive into the science behind ADHD, unraveling its mysteries and discovering how your extraordinary mind works.

Prepare to unleash your superpowers and embark on an adventure that will forever change how you perceive yourself and your potential. Get ready to don your cape and mask, embracing the champion within you—an ADHD superhero ready to conquer the challenges and shine brighter than the sun.

What Is ADHD?

ADHD, or Attention-Deficit/Hyperactivity Disorder, is a neurodevelopmental disorder that affects both children and adults. It is usually first documented in childhood, but the symptoms can continue into adulthood.

Hannah Bookbinder

How Common Is ADHD?

ADHD is found in 11% of school-aged children.[1] Worldwide, approximately 7.2% of children ages eighteen and younger have ADHD.[2] In fact, as of 2020, over 366 million adults had ADHD worldwide, costing our country over $120 billion because of unemployment, lack of productivity, and health care services.[3]

INTERESTING FACT:

Doctors first documented children who struggled with inattentiveness, impulsive behavior, and hyperactivity in 1902. Initially labeled "minimal brain dysfunction," this cluster of symptoms has gone through multiple label iterations, the most recent of which is Attention Deficit Hyperactivity Disorder. This name more accurately reflects the inattentive, hyperactive, and impulsive behaviors associated with this disorder.[4]

---

[1] CHADD, "Overview of ADHD," CHADD: The National Resource on ADHD, accessed September 23, 2024, https://chadd.org/about-adhd/overview/.
[2] CHADD, "General Prevalence," CHADD: The National Resource on ADHD, accessed September 23, 2024, https://chadd.org/about-adhd/general-prevalence/.
[3] "ADHD Statistics," *Forbes*, accessed September 23, 2024, https://www.forbes.com/health/mind/adhd-statistics/#:~:text=An%20estimated%203.3%20million%20U.S.,have%20ADHD%20as%20of%202020.
[4] Michael R. Kohn, Leanne S. Clarke, and Vaughan J. Casey, "Assessing the Efficacy of a School-Based Intervention Program for Adolescents with ADHD," *ADHD Attention Deficit and Hyperactivity Disorders* 2, no. 1 (2010): 41–48, https://doi.org/10.1007/s12402-010-0045-8.

Even more intriguing is the following notion: Psychiatrist Ned Hallowell emphasized that ADHD is a bit confusing because so many people who have it can hyper-focus on subjects they find interesting, but they struggle to focus on less-appealing tasks.[5]

How Is ADHD Diagnosed?

A mental health professional (usually a licensed psychologist, a neuropsychologist, or a medical doctor with expertise in diagnosing and treating ADHD) observes and interviews the individual. The professional also interviews family members and teachers in the form of surveys, including the Connors' Parent Rating Scale, the Vanderbilt ADHD Parent Rating Scale, and others.

This professional uses guidelines from the American Psychiatric Association Diagnostic and Statistical Manual of Mental Disorders to determine whether the patient has ADHD and, if so, the precise type. Specific criteria must be met to be diagnosed. Please see the Appendix for more information.

I Heard There Are Different Types Of ADHD. Is This True?

People with ADHD struggle with focus and attention, impulsivity, and hyperactivity, but it's important to note that this disorder doesn't

---

[5] "ADHD and Hyperfocus: The Fascinating Connection," *ADDitude*, accessed October 14, 2024, https://www.additudemag.com/adhd-symptoms-hyperfocus-attention/.

always manifest the same way for each person. There are three notable forms of ADHD: inattentive, hyperactive, and combined.

Being cognizant of details and checking work for mistakes are frequently elusive tasks for the ADHD brain. Individuals with inattentive ADHD find it difficult to pay attention. With the hyperactive form of ADHD, individuals have a difficult time sitting still, so they are often in perpetual motion, squirming in chairs and bouncing their knees or fidgeting their fingers. Finally, the combined type of ADHD sees a manifestation of both the inattentive and the hyperactive types of this disorder.

How Does ADHD Impact a Person's Life?

While having ADHD is not the end of the world, it certainly poses many challenges for the individual living with the disorder. From an academic perspective, people with ADHD may struggle to hand in work on time—or they may be confused by or even be unaware of due dates.

Since the COVID-19 pandemic, many schools and teachers require students to submit work virtually and, for some students, that's a huge undertaking, considering the multitude of ways in which a student is asked to submit work. Navigating the submission portal, uploading work, and remembering to hit send can frustrate even the most organized of students. For the ADHD kid, it can be a logistical nightmare.

Often, organization eludes an ADHD student. Backpacks are full of nearly-recycled papers, scrunched beyond recognition, and pens and pencils are frequently lost. Remaining motionless and focusing quietly are sometimes next to impossible, so you can bet that sitting still for an exam is difficult. But often, students who have these difficulties are too embarrassed to stand at the back of the classroom to stretch their legs—or worse than that, their teachers have insulted them one too many times when they've asked to walk down the hall to get a drink of water—even if this is a formal accommodation in their IEP, 504, or personal education plan. And to top it all off, ADHD students often have the impulsive desire to call out during the teacher's lesson because they have a question or want to add to the discussion. However, sometimes the risk of humiliation is too great. Instead, they sit and wait as the minutes on the clock tick slower and slower until they can finally be excused, only to start the process all over again in the next classroom.

The struggle to live with ADHD also extends to social relationships. Anyone sitting in that classroom with the kid I just described knows he or she may be met with ridicule. Unless this kid is viewed as "cool" despite his impulsivity, he is an easy target for his peers.

Kids, no matter their age, do not take kindly to peers who constantly engage in what appears to be attention-seeking behavior. They don't like the disruption and the impact it has on the teacher because, let's be honest, if this goes on long enough, the teacher gets angry with the disruptive kid, and sometimes, the teacher takes it out on the whole class. When that happens, you can imagine the greeting that child may receive in the hallway or at recess... it isn't pretty. Consequently, making and keeping friends is often difficult for kids with ADHD.

Are these the challenges you face daily? Confronted with the wrath of teachers, in addition to the frustration and mockery of your peers, school may feel extremely unsafe. Plus, the torture may continue after school because as soon as you set foot in the door, your parents may confront you about your missing assignments, your poor test performance, or your disruptive behavior in class. All this adds up to you feeling defeated and depleted, with no one to turn to for support or validation because no one understands you.

In situations like this, children often turn to behaviors they believe will help them cope. Unfortunately, substance abuse is common among kids struggling to manage ADHD. According to Timothy Wilens, Associate Professor of Psychiatry at Harvard Medical School and Chief of the Division of Child and Adolescent Psychiatry at Massachusetts General Hospital, children with ADHD are more than twice as likely to develop a substance-use disorder compared to their peers without ADHD.[6]

Interestingly, these kids are not seeking to get high as much as they are trying to cope with their mood, get better sleep, or deal with the rejection and shame they experience on any given day. According to Wilens, for students where medication is appropriate, treatment reduces the likelihood of substance abuse by 60%.[7] While this is a strong case for stimulant medications, it doesn't directly address the emotional distress that many individuals with ADHD experience daily.

And that, my dear friend, is why I wrote this book—to empower you with information about your ADHD and to give you strategies to overcome the obstacles you face.

---

[6] Timothy E. Wilens, M.D., "Treating a Child with ADHD Medication Diminishes His Future Risk of Substance Abuse," *ADDitude*, last modified May 22, 2024, from the webinar "ADHD and Substance Use Disorders: How to Recognize and Manage Addiction in Adults and Adolescents," https://www.additudemag.com/adhd-and-substance-abuse-stimulant-medication/.

[7] Timothy E. Wilens, M.D., "ADHD and Substance Abuse: The Link & How Stimulant Medication Can Help," *ADDitude*, accessed October 16, 2024, https://www.additudemag.com/adhd-and-substance-abuse-stimulant-medication/#footnote1.

STOP and Think: What is one fact I just learned in this section?

_____
_____
_____
_____
_____
_____
_____
_____
_____
_____

The News is Not All Bad:

It's true—ADHD poses several challenges. However, after working with this population for more than two decades, I've learned that the ADHD mind is brimming with gifts and talents. Unfortunately, many of these go unrecognized because life with ADHD is an ever-changing landscape, full of last-minute upsets, heated debates with parents, and plenty of unpredictability.

But here's the thing. As I previously mentioned, so many students with ADHD have a unique knack for thinking outside the box. They view situations from a perspective few people can see. For example, one of my students was struggling to prioritize her to-do list. She couldn't conceptualize a way to separate the most pressing tasks from those that were less important. Simply listing them made it even more confusing, and she realized she needed a strategy to visually differentiate between them. Tapping into her artistic background, she created a color-coded system to manage her time and tasks more efficiently, with each color representing a different activity or priority.

For instance, she used a red sticker to mark urgent tasks, a yellow sticker to identify important but non-urgent tasks, and a green sticker to denote less urgent tasks. By using this color-coded system, she could easily glance at her schedule or to-do list and prioritize her tasks based on color. This visual and intuitive approach helped her stay organized and better manage her time, catering to the combination of her organizational needs *and* her creativity.

Here's another example of creative problem-solving: I coached a college freshman who was easily distracted. One of the greatest culprits was his cellphone, but he didn't feel comfortable leaving his device in the common room because a few personal items had already been stolen earlier in the semester, so he insisted on keeping it with him.

Knowing the phone would distract him, he knew he needed to limit the enticement of this device. After much debate, he set his phone to airplane mode. Low and behold, that did the trick! He could keep his phone by his side while simultaneously disabling the very features that pulled him off course. Genius!

STOP and Think: What are my personal benefits of having ADHD?

_____

_____

_____

_____

_____

_____

_____

_____

_____

_____

_____

Is There Anything Else I Need to Know?

It may be interesting to know that some individuals with ADHD also have other challenges. Here are some examples.

Anxiety is a common co-existing diagnosis. According to the Centers for Disease Control and prevention, approximately four out of ten children who have ADHD also have anxiety.[8] This comorbidity should not come as a surprise, given the scenarios we just read about. Anyone who is being met with failure, rejection, ridicule, and self-doubt is susceptible to bouts of anxiety, however benign or gripping. In this book, we will explore the relationship between anxiety and

---

[8] Centers for Disease Control and Prevention, "Data and Statistics About ADHD," *CDC*, last reviewed September 20, 2022, https://www.cdc.gov/adhd/data.

ADHD and identify some helpful strategies to address these challenges.

Perfectionism also accompanies ADHD and anxiety. Students believe if they can just deliver the perfect amount of work with flawless content and performance, everything will be—well—perfect! And yet, that isn't what happens. It only takes one sentence to bring everything to a screeching halt, and everything goes to hell in a handbasket. You can't get the words to sound right; you know what you want to say, but the gap between your mind and your hands feels impossible to bridge. We'll explore these perfectionist tendencies and learn how to embrace the concept of "good enough."

Dishonesty and ADHD can go hand in hand. It makes sense, doesn't it? Why would you share anything that might make you feel even more vulnerable than you already do?

For example, let's say Mom asks you about your English essay. You tell her it's almost done, even though you haven't even started because you anticipate that writing it will take at least five hours, and how the heck are you supposed to endure that form of torture? So, you stretch the truth, and she thinks you're on the right track. Bullet dodged, right?

But then, fast forward a week, and she checks the school grade portal only to see that same assignment is missing. When she asks you about it, you say you submitted it, but there was a glitch in the computer system. You tell her you already spoke with the teacher, and he's letting you resubmit it for full credit.

Pretty soon, that one little exaggeration grows more and more intricate until you are caught in your own sticky mess, with nowhere to hide. This is not uncommon, and we will discuss *why* students utilize dishonesty and explore ways to avoid the very situations that entice students into those slippery tunnels of deception.

Resignation often accompanies ADHD because self-advocacy or asking for help doesn't come easily to neurodivergent kids. Sometimes, it's a matter of personal pride: the child wants to figure things out for himself. Why shouldn't he? He knows he is smart and capable.

If you consider the scenario we imagined in your classroom, why would you ask for help from a teacher who just humiliated you in front of the entire class? No way. It feels better to save face and figure it out on your own, right? After all, you probably should know the answers already... it's not rocket science, right?

That may be true in some cases, but when trying to solve things on your own hasn't worked, there's always another option. Let's explore those options and identify the strategies that will work best for you.

Conflict often arises in relationships with parents as a result of ADHD, and it's one of the greatest and most common challenges kids with ADHD face. It makes sense, doesn't it? If a child is struggling to succeed in school, any good parent would want to jump in and help. While parents may have the best of intentions, sometimes their approach doesn't work for their child.

Some kids need the chance to figure things out for themselves, while others welcome assistance. Constantly harassing a child is never beneficial and can actually increase anxiety. Depending on the student's age, communication between parents and teachers can be helpful, but too much involvement can be overwhelming—for the student *and* the teacher. We will discuss establishing healthy boundaries that promote student independence while also allowing for appropriate levels of parental support.

STOP and think: Do I struggle with any of these additional challenges? If so, which ones and how do they impact me academically, socially, or emotionally?

_____

_____

_____

_____

_____

_____

_____

_____

_____

_____

There was a lot to process in this chapter. In the pages to come, I promise to keep the format brief and to the point. My aim is to use bite-sized chapters with bullet-pointed information so you can use less energy on focusing and more energy where it matters—creating a system of organization and troubleshooting that works for you.

Key Takeaways: Chapter 1

✓ **ADHD is not a limitation** but a unique cognitive wiring that brings with it diverse learning profiles, just like superheroes possess their own extraordinary abilities.
  - Your ADHD superpower may include hyper-focus—the ability to immerse yourself in a task or subject that captures your interest, allowing you to see patterns and solutions that others might miss.
✓ **ADHD affects people in different ways**, with three notable forms: inattentive, hyperactive, and combined. Each type comes with its unique challenges and strengths.
  - The inattentive type struggles with focus and attention, often finding it difficult to prioritize tasks.
  - The hyperactive type has a hard time sitting still and may exhibit fidgeting or restlessness.
  - The combined type experiences a mix of both inattentive and hyperactive symptoms.
✓ **ADHD can present challenges in academic settings**, including difficulties with time management, organization, and focus. However, strategies can be developed to overcome these hurdles and better manage academic responsibilities.
  - Visual cues and color-coded systems can help with prioritizing tasks and managing time efficiently.
  - Technological features like airplane mode can minimize distractions and help maintain focus.
✓ **ADHD can co-occur with other challenges,** such as anxiety and perfectionism. Understanding these additional factors can

provide insights into managing ADHD-related difficulties effectively.

- About four out of ten children with ADHD also experience anxiety, given the daily struggles and potential for rejection and self-doubt.
- Overcoming perfectionist tendencies by embracing the concept of "good enough" can help prevent unnecessary self-imposed pressure.

✓ **Self-advocacy and seeking appropriate support are vital skills** for individuals with ADHD. Finding a balance between independence and seeking assistance can help you navigate challenges more effectively.

- Recognizing when you need help is the first step. Learning to ask for help when needed and utilizing available resources can make a significant difference in your success.
- Establishing healthy boundaries with parents and educators can promote independence while ensuring appropriate support systems are in place.

Chapter 2
The Anxious Hero: Conquering Anxiety and Achieving Academic Excellence

Welcome to the chapter where I lay it on the line. In this chapter, we'll explore the dynamic between anxiety and academic excellence. This chapter will provide you with valuable insights to help you identify your anxiety triggers, gain insight into their meaning to you, and devise a plan of action that will enable you to thrive emotionally and academically.

Remember, anxiety may cast a shadow, but it does *not* define you. Instead, it presents an opportunity for growth and transformation. By harnessing your inner strength, building resilience, and developing coping mechanisms, you will emerge as the hero of your academic journey—fearless, focused, and ready to face any challenge that comes your way.

Can You Relate?

Your history teacher just assigned a major research project:

- Minimum ten pages
- Seven resources—four of which need to be primary, and no, you cannot use Wikipedia.
- You create your own prompt
- Your grade on this paper counts for 30% of your class grade.

This is a disaster. Ten pages?!?! How are you supposed to come up with enough information to fill ten whole pages? Seven resources? Where will you find four primary sources? You need more guidance— why can't the teacher give you the prompt so you can just answer it? This is going to take forever. What if your topic is stupid? What if your paper isn't great? The more you think about this, the more anxious you become. And suddenly, the wheels of production come to a screeching halt.

STOP and Think: Can I relate to this scenario? What causes me the most anxiety in my life? School? Family? Friends? Other?

_____

_____

_____

_____

_____

_____

_____

_____

_____

_____

_____

STOP and Think: What do I usually do to help relieve anxiety?

_____
_____
_____
_____
_____
_____
_____
_____
_____
_____

What's all the fuss about? Why do we build ourselves into such a frenzy, knowing that doing so undercuts our ability to reach our potential? It's important to recognize that anxiety is not based on logic. People do not *choose* to become anxious. This emotion usually comes from a failure to process our primary emotions—hurt, sadness, anger, fear, excitement, happiness, and surprise, to name a few.

Students often experience anxiety about their work due to a variety of factors. First, the pressure to succeed academically can create a sense of dread about meeting high expectations. The fear of failure or receiving poor grades can intensify anxiety, as students may worry about their future prospects and the impact on their self-esteem.

Additionally, the overwhelming volume of assignments, looming deadlines, and the need to balance multiple responsibilities can contribute to a sense of being overwhelmed. The fear of not being able to meet these demands or falling behind can further heighten anxiety.

Furthermore, the perpetual comparison to peers can fuel self-doubt. Students may also experience anxiety surrounding presentations, exams, or public speaking, fearing judgment or criticism from their peers and teachers. The trepidation of making mistakes and the potential consequences of those mistakes can also generate anxiety.

In the world of ADHD, anxiety can be a constant companion because of the unique challenges and demands individuals with ADHD face. The symptoms of ADHD, like focus issues, impulsivity, and hyperactivity, can lead one to feel unsettled and worried. The struggles with staying organized, managing time effectively, and completing tasks can create an overwhelming sense of uncertainty, which can contribute to anxiety.

Additionally, the prospect of repeatedly facing academic and social difficulties, such as poor performance in school or difficulties in interpersonal relationships, can lead to self-doubt and the fear of being judged or perceived as different. The constant need to navigate a fast-paced and often demanding world while grappling with ADHD can create a sense of pressure and anxiety.

However, it's important to remember that anxiety accompanying ADHD is common, and with proper support, strategies, and self-care, you can learn to manage your anxiety—and thrive. So, let's get down to it already. Here are some suggestions for preventing and managing your anxiety.

Strategies

You can find the pdfs for this material on my website: www.mytoadapp.com/chapter2.

One of the most empowering steps you can take to address your anxiety is being proactive. Sometimes, just by the virtue of planning ahead, you give yourself the opportunity to avoid obstacles that will otherwise trip you up and prevent you from meeting your goals. Many of my students complain that taking this initial step is daunting and creates more work than is necessary. But think about this: if you dive into your work without planning out your time or approach, you'll likely end up spending more time and energy on that *one* task than if you'd just taken fifteen minutes to map out a strategy. Imagine how different your levels of anxiety would be!

Consider these time management and organization strategies; they just might be the difference between an anxiety-riddled evening and one that is calm, cool, and collected.

Create a Weekly Spreadsheet that includes your sleep and wake hours, class times, homework periods, and any other daily commitments. Be sure to add in social obligations, extracurricular activities, exercise, and any other tasks you want to track. Google Sheets, Google Calendar, and the *Master Calendar* feature in My TOAD App™ are excellent tools for this purpose. Creating a consistent routine is important for planning but also for creating comfort with a sense of structure and predictability.

	Monday	Tuesday	Wednes-day	Thursday	Friday	Saturday	Sunday
8 am	Wake up	Wake up	Wake up	Wake up	Wake up	Wake up	Wake up
9 am	Break-fast	Break-fast	Break-fast	Break-fast	Break-fast	Break-fast	Break-fast
10 am	Study	Class	Study	Class	Study	Work-out	Work-out
11 am	Class	Group project	Class	Work-out	Class	Group Pro-ject	Study
12 pm	Lunch	Lunch	Lunch	Lunch	Lunch	Lunch	Lunch
1 pm	Stud-ent govern-ment	Study	Study	Stud-ent govern-ment	Yoga	Study	Study
2 pm	Class	Work-out	Class	Work-out	Class	Study	Study

When creating your spreadsheet, be intentional about not only *when* you're going to work, but *what* you are going to do during that time.

Wednesday 9/13/24	Time	Goal
Math	3:30-4:30	Complete problems 1-15 odd
Social Studies	4:45-5:30	Read Section 1 Ch 12 and take notes about the causes of the Civil War
English	None	
Chem	6-7	Write intro and process sections of lab report
Spanish	7:15-8:15	Watch YouTube Foods Video and make a recipe for Tacos Rancheros

Create a Sense of Time by playing Beat the Clock. Set out to complete a task, but prior to doing so, guestimate the time it will take you to complete it. Start your timer and engage in the task. When completed, check to see how long it *actually* took you. How accurate was your prediction? Try it again, but this time, try to use your newly found time savvy to beat the clock! The *Time Estimator* feature in My TOAD App™ walks you through this strategy and helps you to develop a strong sense of time.

Chunk Your Work into Smaller Pieces and schedule them into your daily calendar, treating each bite-size piece of work as you would a daily assignment.

Task	Start Date	Completion Date	Done?
Look at resources.	1/24	1/26	Yes
Write thesis.	1/27	1/28	Yes
Create outline.	1/29	2/1	Yes
Write intro paragraph.	2/2	2/3	Yes
Write section about impact on children.	2/4	2/6	Yes
Write section about impact on social status.	2/7	2/9	Yes
Write section about politics.	2/10	2/12	
Write section about implications for national security.	2/13	2/15	
Write conclusion.	2/16	2/18	
Edit.	2/19	2/22	

Sit and Buckle Up. If you prefer to finish your work in one sitting, try committing to timed chunks. Start with ten minutes, then gradually increase to twenty, thirty, forty-five, or more. Listen to your body— when you feel restless or lose focus, take a short break to walk, have a drink, or grab a snack, and then dive back in.

Organize Your Workspace. Make sure you have everything you need *before* you start to work. Here are some items you may want to consider having in your work area:

- Proper lighting
- Comfortable seating
- Appropriate work area-desk, lap desk, standing desk
- All binders/folders
- Notebooks
- All necessary hard-copy materials (i.e., handouts, worksheets, etc.)
- Access to all digital materials (i.e., folders with your documents)
- Computer
- Calculator
- Pens/Pencils/Erasers/Highlighters
- Flashcards
- Stapler/Paperclips
- Sticky Notes
- Snack
- Water
- Fidgets
- Music/sound maker, if desired

Manage Your Materials. Everything you need has a home. Whether you're using folders, binders, notebooks, or two-pocket folders, they all belong in your backpack. Additionally, it's important to keep items like writing utensils, a calculator, highlighters, sticky notes, and any other essentials in your backpack. A checklist of these items may be helpful as you travel to and from home. You can keep this checklist at the front of a binder, on your locker door, or in another easily accessible spot.

Establish a Homework Protocol. Know *what* is due and what DONE looks like. To do this, note *when* your assignments are due, and be aware of *how* to submit the assignments. Then, confirm you have submitted it, and check the assignment off when it is complete. One surefire strategy you can use is asking your teacher for an example of a solid-A project from a previous class. The idea is not to copy the assignment, but it *will* help you have a point of reference to better understand what DONE looks like.

Establish Homework Management. If you struggle with understanding, completing, and submitting your homework, try using one of these systems:

Double-Check System- After following the homework protocol listed above, place a checkmark next to each assignment. Place a second checkmark next to that same assignment when you have submitted it or placed it into its proper binder/folder.

Assignment	Submission Method	Submitted?
Shakespeare Essay	Turnitin.com	Yes

Homework Board- Using a dry-erase board, create a table using the following labels:

	English	History	Math	Science	Language
Assignment					
Date Assigned					
Due Date					
My Date to Start					
My Date to Complete					
Completed?					
Submitted?					

Transportation of Homework- Use a two-pocket homework folder.

- Label the left pocket "TO HOME." Label the right pocket "TO SCHOOL."
- Remove your homework from your left pocket and complete the assignments.
- Return all completed work to the right pocket.

Backpack Patrol- Set aside time to clean out your backpack nightly, or at least weekly, when you have completed your homework.

- Throw out old food. (You don't want the cure for a disease growing in the bottom of your bag!)
- File all loose papers in their appropriate folder or section in a binder.
- Sharpen your pencils.
- Give your parents any forms they need to sign.

STOP and Think: Of all the proposed strategies, which ones might seem workable for me?

_____

_____

_____

_____

_____

_____

_____

_____

STOP and Think: Identify at least two strategies you want to try.

_____

_____

_____

_____

_____

_____

_____

_____

_____

_____

_____

_____

STOP and Think: What will be your plan of implementation to put these steps into place?

_____

_____

_____

_____

_____

_____

_____

_____

_____

_____

It's important to be proactive *before* anxiety becomes overwhelming. Proactivity means you're taking preventive measures regarding your mental health. Here are some strategies to help you accomplish that.

Deep Breathing

- Find a quiet place to sit or stand.
- Place your hands on your belly.
- Find a focal spot in front of you or close your eyes.
- Inhale and exhale, using a normal pace—not too deep and not too shallow, just the pace with which you normally breathe.
- Be aware of the rising and falling of your stomach muscles with every inhale and exhale.
- Practice this for one minute each day; then extend it to two minutes, building up tolerance for as long as you enjoy.

Here is a variant:
- Inhale through your nose for a count of four.
- Hold for a count of seven.
- Exhale through your mouth for a count of eight.
- Repeat the entire cycle ten times.

Sometimes, deep breathing is not tangible enough, so students need something more concrete. If this is the case for you, try one of these mindfulness exercises:

Mindfulness Exercises

Location Exercise
- Look around you—this exercise can be used anywhere—in your room, in your classroom, outside, on a walk, on an airplane, etc.
- Locate six red things, five orange things, four yellow things, three green things, two blue things, and one purple thing.

Variant: You can use other categories to identify items: six desserts, five entrees, four vegetables, three fruits, two breads, and one fat. Or, think of six NFL teams, five NHL teams, four NBA teams, three MLS teams, two MLB teams, and one tennis player.

The point of this exercise is to give you something concrete to focus on to quiet the noise that can frequently fill your mind.

Ice Cube Exercise
- Take an ice cube and observe it using your five senses:
  - Smell- What does it smell like? (Hopefully, nothing—otherwise, someone may need to clean out your freezer!)
  - Touch- What's the temperature? Smooth or rough? Sharp or round edges?

- o Sight-What does it look like? Bubbles frozen inside? Shape? Size? Clear or cloudy?
- o Hearing-Yes, sometimes ice makes noise! Lift the cube to your ear and have a listen!
- o Taste- Ideally, your ice cube does not taste like anything! But place it in your mouth and observe what happens to the ice cube. How does its shape, size, and texture change? How does your mouth respond to the ice cube's presence? Do you have the urge to bite it? Don't! Hold it in your mouth until it melts.

The point of this exercise is to give you something concrete to focus on to quiet the noise that can frequently fill your mind.

Separation of Work and Play

Try to create a separate workspace from your living space. If quarters are tight, this may be difficult to do, but it can be helpful to carve out a work area that differs from the place where you relax and have fun.

Dorm room- Cordon off a corner of your room that's allocated for your desk or sitting area. Maybe it's possible to loft your bed so the workspace is under your bed—out of sight, out of mind! Try working in the common room, a study space in the dorm, or a library on campus. Keep your relaxation space calm with low lighting, comfortable fabrics for seating and bedding, and soothing colors. Add music or ambient noise and consider the use of essential oils to promote tranquil surroundings.

Bedroom- Follow this same idea, setting aside a distinct area for you to work, preferably as far from your bed as possible. If your home allows for it, set up a workspace at the kitchen or dining room table, a corner of your parent's office, or a spot in your family room. Using the guidelines above, make your relaxation space calm.

Outside Areas- Areas apart from your home offer a multitude of options, depending on your level of distractibility. Libraries offer quiet rooms in which noise is not permitted. Coffee houses always play host to working-minded customers. Join a friend at their home. Work outside at a picnic table at a local park. Visit a local museum and find a quiet nook. The options are endless!

Stress-Relieving Activities

Explore Yoga- Get your downward dog into action. There are plenty of local classes that you can attend in your community and even more options on sites like YouTube. My favorite online instructor is Adriene Mischler. You can find her channel at youtube.com/yogawithadriene.[9] She offers a wide range of yoga practices to viewers of all shapes, sizes, and abilities. Plus, you don't have to invest a lot of time to benefit from practicing with her.

Journal- For those of you who find comfort in writing, journaling can be a therapeutic and calming practice. Think of your journal as your best friend: you can tell it anything, and it won't abandon you. It can keep your most vulnerable thoughts safe and confidential. It gives you the opportunity to reflect on your day, on a relationship, on a problem, etc. If writing or typing your thoughts is too labor intensive, try dictating your thoughts using speech-to-text software on your computer or your phone.

Brain dumps- This is one of my favorite activities. In fact, I find it so valuable, I included a *Brain Dump* feature in My TOAD App™! Sit down with a piece of paper and a pen or pencil. Set a timer for two to

---

[9] Yoga With Adriene, *Yoga With Adriene* (YouTube channel), accessed October 16, 2024, https://www.youtube.com/yogawithadriene.

three minutes and write down everything going through your mind. From the sublime to the ridiculous, every thought is fodder for this exercise... just dump it. If you're thinking about a ladybug, write ladybug. Dessert? Write it down. An argument you had with your best friend? List it. There are no rules for this exercise. You can use bullet points, full sentences, or everything in between. Just get it all out. As an added bonus, sometimes the contents of these dumps can help you create get-to-do lists, organize yourself, or prioritize activities.

Exercise- Bring out your inner Caitlin Clark or Tyrese Maxey and sweat! Those endorphins you feel coursing through your veins as you run, swim, bike, ski, and skate will help to lift your mood and energize your mind and body. In return, this lift will enable you to better focus and organize.

Quiet your inner bully- This will help you lower the volume of self-doubt. We all have one—that nagging inner critic who constantly barks orders, cuts us down, and undermines our ability to succeed. It's time to name this voice. Go ahead; choose a name that works for you, something that really reflects the negativity and torment the bully creates. I named mine Daphne. She's a doozy, constantly nipping at my heels and reminding me of how insecure I feel. She often makes me feel guilty about how I handled a situation, even though I addressed the situation appropriately because I was looking out for myself when no one else was! Shut that voice off! Here's how:

Cognitive restructuring is a powerful tool to challenge and reframe anxious thoughts. Have you ever said this to yourself? "If I don't get an A on this exam, I'll never get into college!" This all-or-nothing way of thinking is enough to make the calmest of people extremely anxious. You're applying too much pressure to the situation and placing too much emphasis on a single outcome. Change the focus to creating a plan of attack. Execute that plan, seeking help when necessary. If you're taking a test, enter the test knowing you did all you could to prepare and feel confident about what you know. You are more likely to meet success with this frame of mind.

Eliminate magical thinking. Stop the belief that an event will cause a particular outcome in an unrelated event. For example, the adage, "Step on a crack and break your momma's back," is silly. If you happen to step on a crack on the sidewalk and your mother breaks her back, that is a remarkable coincidence. You can only control what you can control, and much of that comes as proactive planning and decision-making to create the outcome you desire. Stick to what actually works and set aside your magic wand.

Mole hills are easier to manage than mountains. Is the situation playing out in front of you really disastrous, or are you making a mountain out of a molehill? Take a step back and look at the circumstances for what they are. Is someone in danger? Are you on the verge of personal or academic failure from which you will never recover? I'd be willing to bet that most times, when we feel overwhelmed, we *can* rebound. Take a deep breath and reassess. What's really playing out before you? Now, make a plan of action.

Everyone has heard the saying about actions speaking louder than words. Unfortunately, when anxiety gets the best of us, our emotions speak to us at a deafening volume—more than our reasoning. Just because our anxiety is telling us that something terrible is playing out—and that we are incapable of handling it—does not make it so. Anxiety puts reasoning out of arm's reach. Again, if we calm ourselves long enough to get an accurate lay of the land, we can probably see the situation for what it is—and tap into our own resources to find a plausible solution.

Walk away. When you notice you're getting frustrated about a particular assignment, project, or task, step away from the situation. Take a break and engage in some form of physical activity like walking, swimming, biking, or performing jumping jacks... anything to get your heart pumping and the blood flowing.

Some of my clients perform the best problem-solving when they remove themselves from the problem and exercise. When you return to your workspace, your mind will be clear, and you will be in a better position to be productive.

Be your own cheerleader. Research has shown that the brain actually believes the ideas and convictions we teach it through our own internal thought processes. That negative self-talk persuades our brains to believe we are totally incapable of achieving our own greatness. Personal goals lay at our feet like a clipped film from a movie on the editor's floor. It's time to stop that self-defeating monologue and replace it with statements that begin with "I am."

- ✓ I am capable.
- ✓ I am strong.
- ✓ I am courageous.
- ✓ I am determined to succeed.

By engaging in these powerful self-affirming statements, our brains begin to believe them, and this positivity triggers conviction, determination, and the sense that anything is possible.

Use humor to stave off anxiety. Humor is a personal matter, and everyone finds different things funny. It's essential to find humor that resonates with you and aligns with your values. Experiment with different comedic styles and techniques to find what brings you joy and alleviates anxiety. Surround yourself with things that make you laugh. Watch comedy shows, read funny books or articles, or follow social media accounts that share humorous content. Incorporate jokes or funny anecdotes into conversations with friends or colleagues. Creating a lighthearted, humorous environment can help shift your focus away from anxiety-inducing thoughts and uplift your mood. You'll be defaulting to laughter in no time!

STOP and Think: Of all the strategies that were proposed, which ones might seem workable for me?

_____
_____
_____
_____
_____
_____
_____
_____
_____
_____
_____

STOP and Think: Identify at least two strategies you want to try.

_____
_____
_____
_____
_____
_____
_____
_____
_____
_____
_____

STOP and Think: What will be your plan of implementation to put these steps into place?

_____

_____

_____

_____

_____

_____

_____

_____

_____

_____

_____

_____

STOP and Think: What do you find comical? Is it a TikTokker? Dancing dogs? Jim Gaffigan? (He's one of my favorite comedians!) Playing a prank on a family member or friend? Identify what tickles your funny bone.

_____

_____

_____

_____

_____

_____

_____

_____

_____

_____

STOP and Think: What are some ways you can bring humor into your life?

_____

_____

_____

_____

_____

_____

_____

_____

_____

_____

_____

GOAL

Goal: Identify three things that make you laugh and weave them into your weekly routine.

_____

_____

_____

_____

_____

_____

_____

_____

_____

_____

Bring in the professionals. When all else fails, it's okay to get help. So many of my students are embarrassed to ask for help because they think they should know the answers. Here's the thing; _no one_ has all the answers. Even the smartest of people must lean on others for support now and then. It's what helps us to ensure we are getting the support and care we need. If you feel your anxiety is out of control and you have tried everything to address it, but nothing is working, it's time to get help. Ask your parent or guardian to make an appointment with your doctor, a therapist, or a psychiatrist so you can get some control over your life. If your trusted adult doesn't know where to turn, speak with your physician for guidance. By working with a professional who is experienced in addressing anxiety, you will gain the tools needed to tame the anxiety and empower you with clarity and calmness.

As we conclude this chapter dedicated to the anxious hero, it's important to reflect on one key idea: anxiety does not define you. Your anxiety can serve as a cue to alert you to how you are feeling. Put your detective cap on, take a deep breath, and look at the situation. What are you feeling? What are the possible culprits that are causing this emotional response? What steps can you take to address them? By implementing the strategies and techniques outlined in this chapter, you have equipped yourself with powerful tools to conquer anxiety and unleash your academic and emotional potential.

Key Takeaways: Chapter 2

- ✓ **Anxiety does not define you:** Remember that anxiety is an aspect of your journey, but it doesn't define your abilities or limit your potential for academic excellence.
- ✓ **Strategies empower you:** By implementing strategies such as organization, time management, mindfulness, cognitive restructuring, relaxation techniques, and seeking support, you gain the power to conquer anxiety and navigate academic challenges.
- ✓ **Self-care is crucial:** Prioritize self-care and nurture your well-being. Take time for relaxation, engage in stress-relieving activities, and cultivate a calm and supportive environment to promote academic success.
- ✓ **Resilience is your superpower:** Embrace your resilience and recognize that every challenge you overcome strengthens you. Your journey may have obstacles, but with determination, you can conquer anxiety and achieve your academic goals.
- ✓ **You are not alone:** Reach out for support from trusted individuals, such as friends, family, or professionals. Remember that many heroes throughout history have faced anxiety and emerged victorious, achieving remarkable feats. Seek inspiration from their stories and find comfort in knowing you're not alone on this journey.

Chapter 3
The Truth, the Lie, and the Unfinished Homework: ADHD's Tangled Web of Deception

I never accuse a client of lying. Doing so would immediately put them on the defensive and reduce the chances of ever hearing the full story. I'm also mindful that, most of the time, there's a valid reason for why they weren't truthful in the first place. You'll notice I'm intentionally avoiding the word 'lie' as I write this chapter.

While the word 'lie' technically describes dishonesty, my experience has shown that using it can spark defensiveness—from both parents and kids. But make no mistake, I know when someone isn't being truthful. When people face serious consequences, they'll do whatever they can to avoid them—even if that means stretching the truth. Still, I believe it's more helpful to look beyond the behavior to understand what led them to that choice in the first place.

What's Really Going On?

I don't believe dishonesty is the source of the problem—rather, it is a symptom of what's really going on with the student. Just as a fever is not the cause of someone's illness, fabrications indicate a greater problem. To illustrate, let's eavesdrop on a conversation between a student and her mother:

Mom: "Honey, I was looking at Schoology today, and it looks like the history paper you wrote hasn't been submitted."

Daughter: "Oh yeah. I handed that in, but the teacher didn't get it, so he's letting me turn it in late for full credit."

Mom: "Wow. That's very generous of Mr. K."

Fast forward one week:

Mom: "Jen, I looked at your grades today, and that history paper is still marked as missing. What's the story?"

Daughter: "Oh, right. I forgot to tell you. Mr. K. said there was a glitch in the computer system, and he can see I submitted it, but he can't see the actual paper. The school district's working on it, and as soon as they get it fixed, it should land in his inbox."

This scenario could go on for weeks, and it may be familiar to many of you reading this chapter. How long the student and her mother choose to drag it out is hard to say, but the point is, the kid clearly did not hand in the assignment; in fact, it's debatable whether she completed the paper at all! The question is why she's not forthcoming about what got her to this point.

And this, my dear reader, is the purpose of this chapter: unraveling the knots of deception to help you handle tricky situations with confidence. You'll get a better understanding of why students might misrepresent the truth and how to avoid falling into those traps. By recognizing what drives dishonest behavior, creating a safe space for honesty, and learning problem-solving skills, you'll be equipped to break free from deception and make choices based on integrity.

Before I can offer you suggestions to avoid engaging in dishonest behavior, you need to understand *why* you do it. Protection is one of the top reasons students resort to deception. If a parent, teacher, or friend doesn't know the ugliness of a situation, then the culprit can get away with it. After all, there can be no punishment or other form of negative consequence if the distressed student can slide under the radar undetected, right? For many kids, the pain of losing privileges— like driving, using digital devices, or hanging out with friends—can feel unbearable. However, as you might expect from your own experiences, losing these privileges often masks deeper, more significant issues beneath the surface. If you dig deeper, the real driving forces and motivations to utilize deceptive tactics become apparent. Let's examine this more closely.

Fear of Failure: Being scared of failing often causes students with ADHD to be deceptive about their academic performance as a protective mechanism. Failure is frequently a constant companion of ADHD.

Time Management: Students don't make enough time to complete assignments, which prevents them from handing in the work on time, let alone at all. The result? A failing grade.

Lack of Attention: If a kid can't pay attention in class, she will likely miss key pieces of information. Missed content will lead to gaps in understanding of material or missed directions. Translation? Failure to perform.

Impulsivity: Kids who struggle to keep it together and maintain control over their behavior are frequently subject to mockery and bullying. The result? A kid who feels like a failure among her peers.

Hannah Bookbinder

With the very real threat of failure nipping at their heels, it makes sense that students would engage in dishonesty as a form of protection. Furthermore, students with ADHD may feel overwhelmed by the demands of schoolwork. This can trigger the fear of disappointment or not meeting expectations, leading to yet another reason to be labeled as failures. Misrepresentations about their performance become a way to avoid facing the possibility of failure or judgment. By presenting a false image of success, they hope to maintain a sense of control and protect their self-esteem.

STOP and think: What do you fear most? Are you afraid of failure?

_____

_____

_____

_____

_____

_____

_____

_____

_____

_____

_____

Shame: The shame that often accompanies ADHD can cause students to misrepresent their academic performance. First, students with ADHD may feel embarrassed about their difficulties in meeting academic expectations, such as completing assignments on time or performing well on tests. After all, they are surrounded by their very successful peers, who outwardly achieve academic greatness regularly. Why can't they? ADHD students may worry about being judged, ridiculed, or viewed as lazy or unintelligent by their peers, teachers, or even themselves. I had a student relay the following incident to me.

My client was in class and didn't understand a concept. When the teacher called on him to discuss the topic, he froze, fearful he'd say the wrong thing—and even more afraid his very-accomplished classmates would laugh at his expense. He took a deep breath, looked at his notes, and offered a theory. The teacher raised his hands in disbelief and mocked his contribution to the conversation, saying, "Even a preschooler would know about this concept! Why don't you? What are you, stupid?"

Needless to say, my client was devastated; it took every fiber of his being to sit and endure the remaining thirty-five minutes of the class, holding back tears of shame and trying to block out the nasty comments his peers shot his way for the rest of the period.

Understandably, for students who have experienced this type of public humiliation, taking creative liberties becomes a way to protect themselves from potential shame and to maintain a façade of competence. Additionally, the pressure to meet societal and parental expectations can intensify the fear of shame, leading students to resort to dishonesty to avoid disappointing others or facing negative consequences. How many of you are motivated by pleasing the adults in your lives? How often have you fallen short of their expectations and felt you had to cover up your shortcomings to avoid disappointing the people you care about most?

Finally, it's important to understand that a student's shame is often rooted in the internalized stigma surrounding ADHD itself. No one chooses to be inattentive, disorganized, time blind, or impulsive. That's abnormal, right? Wrong! As the statistics in the introduction demonstrate, ADHD is not so uncommon. But as is true with any struggle or challenge, what is foreign is frequently subjected to dissection and misunderstanding. And therein lies one of the greatest causes of shame for a person with ADHD.

STOP and think: Can you relate to this incident of humiliation? Do you have a similar story? What happened? How did you feel about it? What, if anything, was done to correct the situation?

_____

_____

_____

_____

_____

_____

_____

_____

_____

_____

Pride: Pride can certainly be a tricky little mischief-maker for kids with ADHD and their academic performance. With their incredible intelligence and unique talents, it's no wonder they want to show the world just how capable and independent they can be.

Most of my clients are bright, intuitive, and masterful—the issue is not their intellectual capability but rather those nagging executive functioning skills that prevent them from meeting their potential. But when those ADHD symptoms throw a little curveball into the mix, pride can rear its stubborn head.

"Hannah, I want to do this on my own... I _should_ be able to do this on my own... I don't want any help." Instead of admitting they might need a little extra support, these determined pathfinders decide to take the treacherous journey of deception, weaving intricate tales of their academic prowess to protect that oh-so-delicate pride. Oh, the lengths they'll go to avoid asking for help or appearing vulnerable! It's like watching a comedic juggling act where they try to keep all the balls in the air without anyone suspecting their hidden struggles.

Perfectionist tendencies are pride's frequent companion. Not only does the student need to traverse this tricky terrain solo, but the product of this journey must be perfect. Many of my students freeze at the prospect of writing a paper or engaging in a long-term project. Why?

- They can't find the perfect words to write the sentence.
- Their thoughts are lining up perfectly in their minds, but they can't articulate them in a verbal or written fashion.
- The font isn't aesthetically pleasing.
- Their work environment isn't set up to their liking.
- They don't understand the directions. Failure to understand one directive is enough to stop this idealist dead in her tracks.

My prideful and precisely driven audience who may be reading this section understands the torment that comes with trying to reach an unattainable standard, as well as the irony that accompanies it. You are the driving force behind this emblem of distinction, and yet you can't stop yourself long enough to look at a situation through a kinder, more compassionate lens.

STOP and think: Are you guiding your life by unattainable standards? What prevents you from offering yourself some grace and latitude for error?

_____

_____

_____

_____

_____

_____

_____

_____

_____

_____

_____

It's important to address fears and provide support to students with ADHD. Doing so will help them develop strategies to manage their challenges and learn that failure is a natural part of the learning process. Creating a supportive and understanding environment can help alleviate the fear of failure and encourage honesty and growth.

If you're going to be expected to be honest about your academic performance, it would stand to reason that we, the trusted adults in your life, need to assist you in setting yourself up for success. How do we achieve this goal? We need to empower you with a tool kit of problem-solving skills.

A kid who feels empowered is prone to feel confident, and a confident kid is inclined to make decisions that will lead to success. Teaching neurodivergent students efficient problem-solving and decision-making skills is crucial for promoting honesty. When students possess these skills, they are better equipped to navigate challenging situations and make informed choices. Here's why this is so important:

Enhanced Understanding: Effective problem-solving skills help students understand the consequences of their actions. By considering various solutions and potential outcomes, students can develop a deeper understanding of the impact of their decisions on themselves and others.

Empowered Decision-Making: When students have a repertoire of problem-solving strategies, they become more confident in their ability to make decisions. This empowerment fosters a sense of responsibility and encourages them to make choices based on honest assessment rather than resorting to dishonesty as a shortcut.

Alternative Solutions: Problem-solving skills provide students with a toolbox of alternative solutions. Instead of relying on falsehoods to avoid challenges, they can brainstorm creative solutions that align with their values and the expectations of their surroundings.

Building Trust: Honesty is the foundation of trust. When students consistently demonstrate honesty and integrity as they navigate difficult situations, they earn the trust and respect of their peers, teachers, and parents. This trust creates a positive environment for communication and support.

Long-Term Consequences: Teaching effective problem-solving skills encourages students to think beyond the immediate moment and consider the long-term consequences of their actions. By weighing the potential outcomes and considering the impact on their relationships and goals, they are more likely to choose honesty as a means of preserving trust and maintaining positive relationships.

Self-Advocacy: Problem-solving skills empower students to be strong self-advocates. They learn to articulate their needs openly and honestly, seeking support or accommodations when necessary. By advocating for themselves, students feel less pressure to resort to dishonesty to conceal their struggles.

Life-Skill Development: Effective problem-solving and decision-making skills are essential abilities that extend far beyond academic settings. These skills will benefit students in various aspects of their lives, helping them navigate challenges and make honest choices based on their values and principles.

By teaching students with ADHD effective diagnostic skills, we provide them with valuable tools that promote honesty and integrity. These abilities empower them to approach challenges with confidence, make informed choices, and create a positive environment built on trust and open communication.

STOP and think: When you encounter difficult situations in your life, what are some of your go-to problem-solving strategies that work for you?

_____

_____

_____

_____

_____

_____

_____

_____

_____

_____

_____

STOP

and think: Would any of those strategies work when you are navigating troubled waters in school?

_____

_____

_____

_____

_____

_____

_____

_____

_____

_____

Okay. So, you understand the importance of problem-solving skills, but how do you implement them? Preventing or solving a difficult situation requires strong communication skills. Whether it's your academic or personal life, living with integrity requires you to feel comfortable with open lines of communication. This starts with you and extends to others, particularly the adults in your life.

Yes, your math teacher may be elusive and difficult to work with. Or your science teacher, who has a great sense of humor, can't explain the Krebs cycle if his life depended on it. However, if you plan to succeed in these classes, you must figure out a way to engage with these teachers. If, after trying to talk with them, you realize these teachers cannot help you, you must find someone else who can.

Fostering open communication between you, your parents, and your teachers is essential for creating a supportive and collaborative learning environment. Here are ten strategies to promote effective communication and cultivate non-judgmental attitudes and active listening.

Establish Regular Check-Ins: Schedule regular opportunities to meet with your parents and teachers to discuss progress, challenges, and goals. This can be in the form of parent-teacher conferences, student-led meetings, or even informal check-ins.

Create a Safe and Welcoming Environment: Partner with your parents to create an inclusive and non-judgmental environment where you will feel comfortable expressing your thoughts, concerns, and ideas. Open dialogue should be encouraged and establish an expectation that all voices will be heard and respected.

Utilize Active Listening: Encourage the use of active listening by providing dedicated time for all parties to express their thoughts without interruption. Encourage paraphrasing and summarizing to ensure understanding and the demonstration of respect for individual perspectives.

Embody Empathy and Understanding: Encourage empathy and understanding among all participants by emphasizing the importance of putting oneself in others' shoes. You, your parents, and your teachers must recognize that everyone may have unique experiences and challenges.

Practice Non-Judgmental Attitudes: Discuss with your parents the detrimental effects of judgment and the benefits of adopting non-judgmental attitudes. You and your parents will need to seek understanding and offer support to one another rather than making assumptions or passing judgments. These conditions and parameters are usually a given in conversations with teachers, so be aware when this is not the case and seek assistance from another teacher, your guidance counselor, a vice principal, or the principal.

Use Active Problem-Solving: Work with your parents and teachers to use problem-solving skills to tackle challenges. Utilize brainstorming and the exploration of different solutions and remember that difficulties are opportunities for growth and collaboration.

Appreciate Diverse Perspectives: The adults you are working with may be "old," in your opinion (Just remember, seventy is the new sixty!). But the years they have under their belts have provided them with a wealth of experience and plenty of opportunity to put many of their now tried-and-true strategies to the test. Looking at a situation from another perspective can prove valuable. Recognize that each participant brings unique insights and experiences to the conversation.

Encourage Openness and Honesty: Being honest, particularly with your parents and teachers, can feel extremely uncomfortable, especially when you're already feeling vulnerable. Your honesty may get you into some hot water, but the temperature will only rise if you aren't candid. As I always tell my clients, in my role as their academic coach, my best help depends on the information they provide me. If they say everything is great academically but they are really failing classes, they deny themselves the opportunity to receive the actual help they need. It's better to share your problems openly rather than hide them, as this allows for early intervention and support.

Focus on Clear and Respectful Communication: If your advisors are going to help you, you must use clear and respectful communication, both in spoken and written forms. Use "I" statements to express thoughts and feelings while maintaining a respectful tone. Before speaking with your teacher, think about what you need from the conversation. For example, if you need more time to prepare for an exam, you could say, "I would appreciate it if you could provide the review materials earlier in the week, so I have more time to study without feeling rushed."

Maintain Collaboration and Partnership: A partnership exists between you and your parents—and you and your educators. After all, you are collectively sharing in the goal of your personal and academic success. Collaborate in the decision-making processes, allowing all parties to have a voice—and actively contribute to finding solutions.

Many of these strategies may feel initially uncomfortable. But if you can see past the discomfort and recognize that these steps will empower you, their implementation can help foster open communication, build stronger relationships, and create a supportive network that benefits your academic and personal growth.

Goal: Which of the strategies that we talked about might you use to increase your use of transparency with yourself and the trusted adults in your life?

_____

_____

_____

_____

_____

_____

_____

_____

_____

_____

_____

SIDE NOTE:

Let's take a minute to talk about one
of my powerful theories.

Good Enough Is Enough

You are your own worst critics; no one can cut you down more effectively than you can. For what it's worth, that doesn't make you special because we all grapple with the same challenge in our lives. At times, you hold yourself to an unreasonable standard, seeking perfection where, often, it just isn't realistic. Like I tell so many of my students, good enough is just that—good enough. Several of my clients set high expectations for themselves, and if they could only become comfortable with their best effort, it would far exceed those of their peers, who are often content with mediocrity.

Your word choices do not have to be perfect *before* you write your essay. The plan of attack for your school project does *not* have to take perfect form before you plan it. Whatever task you are about to embark on is not a doctoral dissertation, and even if it were, your readers and advisors make allowances for error.

I'm not telling you to abandon the notion of putting forth your best effort, but I am suggesting you offer yourself some grace and allowance for minor blemishes. Lower the temperature a bit and give yourself the opportunity to experience the learning process as it was meant to be—with the aim of discovery and exploration. Worry less about your preconceived notion of what "good" is because if you are truly feeling confident, everything else will fall into place.

Now that we have established the importance of problem-solving strategies and the communication skills needed to execute them, let's discuss the actual skills themselves.

Utilize Chunking: Break down complex problems or tasks into smaller, more manageable steps. This method makes tasks feel less overwhelming and promotes steady progress. For example, you may have a major history exam coming up, but you don't know where to begin. Look through the chapter, paying attention to the titles and subtitles. Divide the chapter into chunks based on these headings. If there are five subtitles, break your study sessions into five sittings. During each session, focus on the bold terms, key questions, important events, dates, concepts, and significant figures within those sections.

Focus on a Step-by-Step Approach: Break each step down further, providing clear instructions on what needs to be done at each stage. This helps maintain focus and clarity throughout the problem-solving process.

Visualize the Process: Use visual aids, such as diagrams, flowcharts, or mind maps to visually represent the steps involved in solving a complex problem. This can enhance understanding and organization.

Consider Consequences: Consider the potential consequences of different actions or solutions. This helps develop critical thinking skills and promotes thoughtful decision-making.

Reflect on Previous Experiences: Reflect on similar problems you have solved successfully in the past. This provides a sense of self-efficacy and a reminder that you possess *actual* problem-solving skills.

Seek Guidance: Reach out for guidance and support when facing complex problems. This can include seeking help from teachers, peers, or experts in the field. Collaborative problem-solving can lead to fresh perspectives and innovative solutions.

Utilize Resources: Utilize resources such as textbooks, online platforms, or reference materials to gain insights and gather information related to the complex problem you are facing.

Break It Down Further: If a problem still feels overwhelming, break it down even further into smaller steps. This systematic approach allows you to tackle one manageable piece at a time until the larger problem becomes more approachable.

Time Management: Develop time management strategies to ensure you allocate sufficient time for problem-solving without feeling rushed or overwhelmed. Breaking down the problem into smaller steps can aid in planning and estimating the time needed for each step.

Reflect and Learn: Reflect on your problem-solving process once you have reached a solution or made progress. This reflection helps you identify what worked well, what could be improved, and what strategies to apply to future challenges.

By utilizing these practical strategies, you empower yourself to approach complex problems systematically, consider consequences, and seek guidance when needed. This comprehensive approach promotes critical thinking skills, resilience, and effective problem-solving abilities, all of which will enable you to feel more confident in your ability to succeed. With your confidence firmly in place, you will be more likely to engage in an ethical, honest pursuit of academic *and* personal success.

STOP and think: Which of these strategies appeals to you?

_____

_____

_____

_____

_____

_____

_____

_____

_____

_____

_____

Goal: Identify two ways you can incorporate them into your daily routine.

_____

_____

_____

_____

_____

_____

_____

_____

_____

_____

Real-Life Example

Several years ago, I worked with a student who consistently fabricated stories. Dishonesty came as naturally to her as breathing; it was *that* easy. More troubling was how easy it was to believe her—she was endearing, bright, and personable. You couldn't help but look into her sweet face and believe everything she said, but in the end, her charm was not enough to hide the truth: she had at least ten missing assignments and had earned 'Ds' on two recent assessments. Eventually, she realized she couldn't maintain this mask; something had to change.

By the time she came to my office, her parents were distraught, and she was ready to put *them* up on eBay. The nightly arguments about missing assignments had taken a severe toll on their relationship. This was very apparent when they met as a family in my office. No one could get a word in edge wise, and even when no one was speaking, I could cut the tension hanging in the air with a knife.

Life was unbearable, and the student was ready to work. We agreed we would begin every meeting with a reflection on the week—what went well and where she felt she needed support. We then checked her grades on the school portal. This information informed the agenda for the rest of our time together.

By placing *her* in the pilot's seat, I empowered her to decide how the time would be used. Furthermore, she saw that I believed in her ability to advocate for herself, which in turn enabled her to believe in herself. With this as the framework for our relationship, she learned to trust me, knowing I would not pass judgment on her, regardless of the infractions she committed.

Don't get me wrong. I most certainly held her accountable for her choices, but I never humiliated her. Instead, we unpacked each situation, identifying what went well and what caused it to go so very wrong. We even explored alternative routes she could take in future situations. Soon, the dishonesty decreased, and the rate of success improved dramatically.

Ten years later, this young woman is now a teacher. Recently, she contacted me to let me know that she proudly and confidently shares the skills she learned from our time together with her own students. She is training another generation of proud, confident, and resilient students to advocate for themselves and engage in their academic journey with integrity.

P.S. She removed her parents from the auction list on eBay, and they now enjoy a healthy relationship, speaking with one another often.

After twenty-five years of working with students of all ages, I am convinced that 99.9% of the time, students misrepresent facts for valid reasons. Whether she's embarrassed about an academic failure, struggling to start an assignment, or unsure how to advocate for herself, there's often a meaningful reason the full story isn't being shared. It's critical to peel away the layers of the situation to understand what's really going on and take steps to address it in a healthy, effective fashion.

Honesty is not just a moral compass; it is a superpower that enables you to build trust, foster authentic connections, and nurture personal growth. So, take out your peeler and identify the issues at hand. Keep your values and integrity intact and unleash the superpower of honesty as you continue to supercharge your ADHD.

Key Takeaways: Chapter 3

✓ **Honesty is a superpower:** Embrace honesty as a superpower that empowers you to build trust, foster authentic connections, and nurture personal growth.

✓ **Understand the reasons behind deception:** Explore the underlying factors that contribute to dishonest behaviors, such as fear of failure, impulsivity, perfectionism, or difficulty with self-advocacy. Cultivate empathy and compassion to understand these reasons and provide support.

✓ **Create a safe and trusting environment:** Foster open communication and non-judgmental attitudes between students, parents, and teachers. Establish clear expectations, provide constructive feedback, and promote a growth mindset that values learning from mistakes.

✓ **Equip yourself with problem-solving skills:** Learn effective problem-solving and decision-making skills to help you navigate challenging situations and make ethical choices. Break down complex problems, consider consequences, and encourage seeking guidance when needed.

✓ **Draw inspiration from others:** Learn from their stories and use them as reminders of the power and impact of honesty in shaping your own life.

Chapter 4
Perfectly Imperfect: Embracing Imperfections to Reach Academic Success

What comes to mind when you hear the word "perfect"?

- Straight lines and rows?
- An A+ paper?
- A snazzy outfit complete with color-coordinated accessories?
- A perfect attendance record?
- Personal athletic performances?

So many of us get caught up in a quest for perfection; after all, if we can achieve that standard, everything else in our lives will be...

well, perfect, right? Ariana Grande once said, "Perfectionism is self-doubt wrapped in pretty packaging." The standard of perfectionism is frequently viewed as an admirable aspiration, but it frequently serves to mask something we want to hide from the rest of the world. Behind that burning hunger to be perfect is a deep sense of insecurity and self-doubt. But we can't let our friends, parents, and teachers know how vulnerable we feel because that would mean we *aren't* perfect.

The underlying message here is the value and importance of embracing imperfection to seek self-acceptance rather than persistently seeking an ideal that is, more often than not, unattainable.

I realize we are entering some uncomfortable and perhaps unchartered waters in this chapter. For my perfectionist readers, you are going to be pushed to look inward and examine the motivation behind your desire for perfection. I will then present you with a kinder and more compassionate lens through which you might look so you can bring some well-deserved self-kindness.

Please understand that I am not encouraging you to lower your standards and resort to failure and despair. On the contrary, my motivation for including this chapter is that I have seen too many students like you struggle to reach a standard that not only is unattainable but drives a significant number of individuals to the brink of a mental-health crisis.

Don't you think it's time to lower the heat under your personal pressure cooker and allow room for empathy and understanding? If you allow yourself that chance, you'll open a new, kinder world of opportunity for academic and personal success.

In this chapter, we will explore the powerful impact of letting go of unrealistic expectations and nurturing a mindset that celebrates progress over perfection. We'll delve into the triggers and detrimental effects of perfectionism. You'll also learn practical techniques to shift your mindset and set realistic goals.

Take a deep breath, quiet the naysayer in your head, and be open to celebrating imperfection and the potential that you'll unlock.

Impact

Some of you may scratch your heads, wondering why we need to talk about the impact of perfectionist tendencies. For many of you, this proclivity motivates you to do well, and it gives you a sense of control over a situation, particularly one that's especially trying.

But here's the thing, this behavior is not really giving you control. Instead, it is likely adding to your stress level, and you are probably so accustomed to feeling this way, you are no longer aware of its toll. If you are going to have any hope of finding the courage to address this beast, you really need to understand the destructive impact it may have on your life. On the other hand, some of you are painfully aware of the powerful impact of these unrealistic standards and seeing them laid out in front of you may validate your experience.

Increased Anxiety and Stress: Perfectionism is no friend to a student. The constant self-imposed pressure to meet unattainable standards, coupled with the terror of making mistakes, can cause excessive worry, self-doubt, and a constant sense of being overwhelmed.

Procrastination and Reduced Productivity: The paralysis that results from the fear of failure is frequently a direct consequence of perfectionist thinking. The inability to establish and maintain traction leads to procrastination tactics, leading to fitful initiation of work and a reduction in overall productivity.

Impaired Time Management: Students with ADHD already face challenges with time management, and perfectionism can exacerbate this issue. The excessive time spent on perfecting tasks can lead to the loss of time allocated to completing other assignments, resulting in missed deadlines, poor grades, and an overall increase in stress.

Negative Impact on Self-Esteem: With these rough waters churning, it's not unusual for students with ADHD to experience a decrease in self-esteem. Constantly falling short of unrealistic expectations can erode confidence, create a negative self-image, and breed a persistent fear of failure.

Reduced Enjoyment of Learning: It makes sense then that existing in this pressure cooker leads to the loss of joy in learning, as an obsessive focus on flawlessness undercuts personal satisfaction. Students may lose interest in subjects they once enjoyed, feel discouraged by setbacks, and experience a diminished sense of curiosity and exploration.

Having just built a solid case for the importance of addressing perfectionist academic tendencies, let's delve more deeply into its causes. If you understand what provokes this destructive behavior, you have a better shot at cutting it off at the pass, silencing your inner idealist, and paving a helpful path to peak academic performance.

Triggers

Loss of Control: I recently worked with a student who has ADHD. He was struggling to start an essay. "I can't get the right words out." He sighed, throwing his pencil onto the desk and lowering his head in defeat. "I want it to be perfect because nothing in this stupid ADHD life of mine is." I asked him to sit up, push the notebook aside, and look me straight in the eye, telling him I thought we needed to unpack what he had just said. After an hour of conversation, this student had unloaded the following thoughts and experiences:

- His ADHD made nearly every task, academic or not, virtually impossible to initiate and complete.
- His distractibility made it difficult to focus on the directions for an assignment, so he was doomed to fail every time.

- Disorganization caused him to lose critically important materials, which meant he frequently failed to hand in his homework.
- Impulsivity wreaked havoc in his social life because no one wanted to hang out with a kid who was out of control.

The list went on and on, and it quickly became apparent that this poor kid felt he had no sense of control or agency in his life. ADHD had robbed him of these very basic human needs. Consequently, at an early age, he engaged in the pursuit of perfectionism. He believed that if he could just reach an ideal standard of performance, he could regain control of his life.

But as we spoke, he had an epiphany and realized that perfectionism was *not* the key to his success. He needed to embrace his own blemishes before he could recognize and ultimately celebrate his strengths, of which there were many.

Family Circumstances: Anyone knows that being a part of a family has its difficulties. Fortunately for a lot of us, our family experiences are mostly positive. However, in some cases, difficult situations can throw us into a tailspin, and in these situations, we are left grasping for any semblance of control. For some, that means launching a quest for perfection. After all, if we can just make sure everything is perfect, then it will all be okay.

Deadlines: Meeting deadlines is a necessary part of being a successful student. However, for some students with ADHD, these due dates can often trigger perfectionist tendencies because the pressure to complete tasks within a specified time frame can intensify their fear of failure. As many of my readers know, getting work done under the best of circumstances is difficult enough—distractibility, disorganization, disrupted thought processes, and poor time management regularly interfere with a student's ability to succeed.

If an assignment is challenging, all the usual obstacles can become exacerbated, resulting in an overwhelmed and paralyzed student. To meet the deadline, they may become excessively focused on perfecting every detail, leading to increased anxiety, self-doubt, and a tendency to procrastinate.

Challenging Assignments: Difficult assignments can cause students with ADHD to resort to perfectionist tendencies because their fear of not meeting the high standards of an assignment is so intense, they will do anything to avoid feeling incompetent. What better way to avoid this potentially humiliating situation than to engage in fastidious behavior, including excessive checking, revising, and striving for flawlessness, which can hinder progress and increase stress levels?

Isn't it interesting to examine how impactful and far-reaching these triggers can be? Watching my students encounter some of these variables is like watching a line of dominos... when one falls, the adjacent domino topples over, forcing the next one to react in kind.

It's time to stop the domino effect, reinforce yourself with some effective strategies, and embark on a new approach to meeting academic and personal success.

STOP and think: Which of these triggers impacts you the most?

_____

_____

_____

_____

_____

_____

_____

_____

_____

_____

_____

STOP and think: How do they impact you?

_____
_____
_____
_____
_____
_____
_____
_____
_____
_____
_____

Strategies

First off, it's important to understand the difference between pursuing excellence and pursuing perfection:

- Pursuing perfection usually translates into setting extremely high standards for oneself that are unforgiving and do not allow for accommodation when they are not being met, whereas pursuing excellence involves high standards that incorporate flexibility when accommodation is necessary.
- A perfectionist views mistakes as indications of failure, whereas someone who pursues excellence views mistakes as an opportunity for growth and learning.
- Perfectionists focus on the _outcome_ (i.e., grades), while pursuers of excellence are able to concentrate on the process _and_ the outcome.

- Fear of failure frequently motivates perfectionists, while optimism and belief motivate pursuers of excellence in their ability to succeed.
- Perfectionists will only be happy if they reach a very unattainable result, while those who pursue excellence can find personal satisfaction with several outcomes.

Using the suggested list of common triggers we discussed earlier in this chapter, identify your own vulnerabilities and use the following list of strategies to create a plan of attack.

Time Management: Break assignments into smaller chunks, schedule each one, and complete them on the assigned date you have given yourself. Use My TOAD App™ to break down your assignments in the *Task Manager* tool and calendar each chunk into the *Master Calendar* tool.

Managing Deadlines: Use an assignment tracking tool and map out your official deadlines (those issued by teachers and professors) and your own personal deadlines. Track your progress using the Homework Tracker sheet we discussed in Chapter Two.

Handling Assignments: Read over the directions, breaking them down into smaller components. What do you need to do first? Second? Third? If there is an aspect of the assignment you do not understand, ask for help from a peer, teacher, professor, or parent.

Learning to Begin: Sometimes, not knowing where to begin provokes our inner critic, and suddenly, we are subjected to some of the harshest judgments we have ever experienced. Take a deep breath; I promise you've got this. Jackson Pollock was a famous abstract impressionist artist. His technique was to dip his paintbrush into a can of paint and flick the paint onto a canvas. Using different colors, he engaged in this process until his canvas reflected something he liked. The same strategy can be used in starting a project, lab report, paper, or presentation. Throw out all your ideas onto the screen or a piece of paper until something takes shape. Once you can visualize your starting point, you can build from there!

Control High-Pressure Situations: First, you must breathe. You have probably been in stressful situations before. How did you handle it? What worked for you, and what didn't? Be kind to yourself and remind yourself of how very capable you are. Just as you peel away the layers of an assignment, so too can you analyze this situation and determine the best steps to resolve it.

- ✓ What is the issue at hand?
- ✓ What concerns you most?
- ✓ What do you feel most comfortable about?
- ✓ What tools and skills do you bring to the situation that will help you to navigate this situation?
- ✓ Who can you turn to for help?

Utilize Your Academic Strategies

- Time Management: Review the strategies we outlined and discussed in Chapter Two.
- Organizational Skills: Think about the plans we explored in Chapter Two.

Unpack Your Fear

- What is causing you so much concern about the situation you are facing?
- Is this fear realistic? Check-in with someone you trust to do a reality check.
- How likely is it to become a reality?
- Are you capable of problem-solving using some strategies we discussed in Chapter Three?

- What are some steps you can take to prevent the outcome that concerns you?

Recognize Your Own Strengths

By now, you are aware of some of the many strengths you possess. Tap into these and use them as you face your fears. Here are some suggestions:

Creativity: Students with ADHD are some of the most creative people I have ever met. Their knack for thinking outside of the box is so incredible to watch as they use imaginative approaches to tackle challenging tasks or discover alternative solutions. Using innovative approaches to situations can help alleviate fears and make the learning process more engaging.

Hyper-focus: ADHD individuals can experience periods of hyper-focus on activities of interest. Using this superpower for desirable activities can serve as the framework for approaching unpleasant tasks. By identifying their passions and creating a structured environment, they can channel this intense focus toward tackling their fears, breaking tasks into manageable steps, and achieving success.

Self-Advocacy: Building a strong support network is crucial, and if you are a confident self-advocate, that's half the battle. Students with ADHD can capitalize on their strong communication skills to discuss their fears and specific needs with teachers, counselors, and family members. Advocating for accommodations can help reduce anxiety and create a more supportive learning environment.

Tech Savvy: Many of you are natural-born techies, able to maneuver through the digital and virtual realms in a seamless and awe-inspiring capacity. (I have learned many of my computer hacks from my own clients!) Technology offers numerous aids for managing ADHD-related challenges. Students can leverage a comprehensive app like My TOAD App™ that improves time management, organization, focus, and accountability. Implementing assistive technology can empower them to tackle their fears more effectively.

Self-Care: Some of you are years ahead of your peers, already recognizing the importance of self-care and the positive impact it can have on your mental health. Kudos to you! As many of you already know, engaging in activities that enhance mental and physical well-being can greatly reduce fear and anxiety. Regular exercise, sufficient sleep, healthy eating, and relaxation techniques like meditation or deep breathing exercises can help students with ADHD stay calm, focused, and better equipped to confront their fears.

Positive Self-Talk: Challenge negative self-talk and perfectionistic tendencies by replacing self-critical thoughts with compassionate and realistic statements. Replace "You are such an idiot! How do you not know this information by now?" with "You have been taking all the right steps to master this material—talking with your teacher, meeting with your tutor, going to study sessions with your friends... just take a deep breath, and try some strategies that have always worked. You can do this!" Breaking the cycle of self-defeating thoughts is key to your success. When you can speak with kindness and compassion to yourself, you will experience calm and clarity, which can lead to productivity and growth.

Mistakes and Setbacks: Think about this: you didn't just roll out of bed at three or four years old and suddenly start to read. You became familiar with the letters and their sounds, sometimes confusing the 'g' sound with the 'j' sound or writing the letter 'd' instead of the letter 'b.' But these mistakes helped you create personal strategies that worked for you, which helped you master the skill of reading. The same principle applies to higher-level tasks. Look at what went wrong and determine what you can do differently the next time you face the same set of circumstances. Not one of us is perfect, no matter what our social media posts might suggest. Making mistakes is part of the human condition, and it is what ultimately makes us better people.

Supportive Network: When all else fails, it is okay to ask for help. As we will establish in Chapter Five, asking for help is a sign of self-awareness and personal strength. Most teachers and professors, especially those who identify students as serious about their academic success, recognize that it takes courage to advocate for oneself. They admire, respect, and celebrate any student who seeks the help they deserve.

Trusted Individuals: Reach out to people you respect, like friends, family, or mentors—people who can provide emotional support and understanding. Consider joining support groups or seeking professional guidance, such as therapy or counseling, to learn additional coping strategies and to gain insights from others.

POINT OF INTEREST:

When a contractor is building a house, his/her first task is to ensure the foundation is solid. It makes little sense to build a beach house directly on the sand, as the ground will shift, and the house will settle at a rate that leaves it vulnerable to collapse.

Any of my students will tell you, I use this analogy often when we are discussing personal well-being. You, dear student, cannot expect to perform well and remain standing if you are not tending to your own foundation, which consists of six pillars: maintaining good sleep hygiene, drinking water and eating a balanced diet, exercising regularly, talking about your feelings, and making time for fun. If one of these pillars is missing from your daily routine, you are as solid as that house built on the sand.

GOAL

Goal: Identify at least two strategies you can use to counter your triggers and create a plan of action for their use.

_____

_____

_____

_____

_____

_____

_____

_____

_____

_____

_____

Many of you are familiar with Simone Biles, the most decorated gymnast of all time. She pulled out of the 2020 Tokyo Olympics to address her mental health. Many praised her decision to prioritize her personal well-being over the anticipated rewards of another sweep of the competition.

In an interview, Biles said, "Walking away from the Olympic Games was a win in itself. I know a lot of people thought I failed because they expected me to go out with five or six medals, but walking out of it was my biggest win.[10]"

_____

[10] Sara Tardiff, "Simone Biles Called Dropping Out of the Tokyo Olympics Her 'Biggest Win,'" _Teen Vogue_, April 14, 2022, https://www.teenvogue.com/story/simone-biles-called-dropping-out-of-the-tokyo-olympics-her-biggest-win.

By seeking support from her team and her mental health professionals, she not only prioritized her well-being, but she inspired others to feel safe and confident to do the same.

Preserving your mental health is an important life skill, and you owe it to yourself to do that now. Society is gradually realizing that mental well-being is just as crucial as physical health.

Conclusion

It's time to break the chains of perfectionism and start embracing a realistic viewpoint, embarking on a journey of self-discovery and growth. Remember, life is not a perfectly choreographed dance; it's a unique canvas waiting for your creative brushstrokes.

Brené Brown, a renowned researcher and author, champions the idea of embracing imperfection and vulnerability as pathways to authenticity and connection. She reminds us that being imperfect is part of being human, and by embracing our shortcomings, we create space for growth, empathy, and self-acceptance. In the realm of academics, this means viewing mistakes as valuable learning experiences, daring to take risks, and celebrating progress over unattainable standards. So, let go of the pursuit of flawless perfection, embrace the beauty of your individuality, and paint your academic canvas with brilliance.

Key Takeaways: Chapter 4

- ✓ **The pursuit of perfection is deceptive:** People often pursue an ideal standard because it gives them a sense of control, which is misleading since this quest sets the navigator up for greater stress and heartache.
- ✓ **Embrace progress over perfection:** Make the distinction between being a pursuer of perfection and a pursuer of excellence. Shift your focus from unattainable ideals to celebrating progress and growth. Recognize that success is not solely defined by flawlessness, but by the effort, improvement, and resilience you demonstrate along the way.
- ✓ **Recognize your triggers and address them:** Knowing what provokes your perfectionist tendencies and being able to address them will help you rein in and stop these destructive tendencies.
- ✓ **Identify strategies to help you manage your desire for perfection:** Find what works for you and use these tricks to empower yourself to shift to a pursuit of excellence.
- ✓ **Learn from mistakes:** Embrace mistakes as valuable learning opportunities. Understand that setbacks and failures are part of the journey and offer insights for improvement. Cultivate a mindset that sees mistakes as steppingstones toward success.
- ✓ **Foster self-compassion:** Be kind to yourself and practice self-compassion. Treat yourself with the same understanding and empathy you would offer a friend. Embracing imperfection means acknowledging that everyone makes mistakes and that perfection does not define self-worth.

✓ **Set realistic expectations:** Set realistic and achievable goals that align with your capabilities and values. Break tasks into manageable steps to avoid becoming overwhelmed by the pressure of perfection. Embrace a growth mindset that values effort and progress rather than fixed outcomes.

✓ **Embrace your uniqueness:** Recognize and celebrate your individuality. Embrace the qualities that make you unique and use them as strengths in your academic pursuits. Embracing imperfection allows you to showcase your authentic self, fostering creativity and a sense of fulfillment.

Chapter 5
Stand Tall and Speak Loud: The Art of Self-Championing

Did you ever have a feeling that gnaws at your mind until it's raw? That gut sense that something just isn't right? Maybe you can't identify the problem, but you just can't find the words to articulate it effectively enough to get the help you need.

Whatever the scenario might be, it's troubling enough to keep you awake at night, tossing and turning, begging for the sun to rise so you can get out of bed and escape this uncomfortable headspace. But then what? Do you choose to seek help, or do you convince yourself to tough it out? You're smart enough; you have the savvy and wherewithal to figure it out... and yet, you just... can't... put... the... pieces... together.

Calming the Frustration

Does this situation feel familiar to any of you? I could sense the tension rising on your side of this book. It doesn't have to be this way. Feeling stuck is extremely frustrating, particularly for a student who has ADHD. Often, the struggle has little to do with intellectual ability; instead, individuals confront numerous scenarios each day that lead to feelings of humiliation because they can't seem to get it together.

A kind-hearted teacher patiently smiles as she tries for the third time to keep her student on track, but she unwittingly reveals her frustration by closing her eyes and breathing deeply in the middle of the classroom. The kid sees it, and so do her peers. ADHD 1: Kid 0.

A bubbly, energetic third grader impulsively calls out an answer, only to realize he is responding to a question the teacher posed two questions ago. The class erupts in laughter, with one of his peers shouting, "Good one, Dylan!" ADHD 2: Kid 0.

A breathless high school junior arrives late to class, huffing and puffing, ready to present his capstone project, but then, he realizes he left his laptop with his entire PowerPoint presentation in the backseat of his car. The teacher smiles and allows him to go back to his car, but he becomes so anxious, he loses his nerve and drives home instead. ADHD 3: Student 0.

With these daily obstacles as the backdrop for students with ADHD, is it a surprise that so many of them feel extremely uncomfortable asking for help? My goal is to change this for you, my dear reader. We will delve more deeply into why you might be so reluctant to ask for help. You'll learn why it is so valuable to advocate for yourself, and you'll explore strategies to help you find your voice, build self-confidence, and effectively communicate your needs.

Included in this conversation will be ways to recognize when you need help, what to ask, who to ask, what to say, and how to determine whether you got the support you needed. You'll learn to navigate difficult conversations, ensuring that you find your voice and effectively advocate for yourself and your needs.

It may be a bit of a bumpy ride at first, but by the end of this chapter, I hope you will identify some techniques to help you confidently embark on your journey of self-advocacy. I want you to empower yourself with the tools to navigate the challenges of ADHD and, ultimately, find greater success and fulfillment in your everyday experiences.

Self-Advocacy

It's okay to ask for help. As we have discussed, a lot of students feel uncomfortable with this. For a variety of reasons, seeking assistance feels extremely uncomfortable. I get it. But let me offer you a different perspective on the topic.

To begin with, when you ask your teachers and professors for help, it gives them the opportunity to spout off about topics they (usually) feel passionate about. World War II? Oh my gosh, your teacher could talk your ear off about Wojtek, the Syrian brown bear that assisted Polish troops—or that Gandhi apparently sent Hitler a letter encouraging him to stop the war.

So, your one gesture actually benefits your teacher, too! More importantly, any teacher who has a solid understanding of what it's like to be a student recognizes the vulnerability that comes with asking for help. They see this solicitation of assistance as an act of courage, not as a sign of weakness, which is widely believed by many students. Your inquiries demonstrate your desire to succeed and your interest in that particular subject.

This, in turn, entices teachers into wanting to help you. For many, they may even be more inclined to throw you a bone when you run late with an assignment because they have witnessed firsthand your hard work and dedication. So, in the end, it's a win-win scenario in asking for help.

One other thought on the subject: in the situation where your teacher really isn't interested in or cannot help you, don't just throw your hands in the air and give up. Find an alternative source of help. Talk with another teacher or professor in another section of the class. Utilize your school's other resources, including writing and math centers and discussion sessions. Discuss the material with your classmates and friends. When all else fails, seek help from an outside resource like a tutor, an academic coach, a family member, or a family friend who has expertise in this particular subject.

STOP and think: How do you feel about asking for help? Is this something you feel comfortable doing?

_____

_____

_____

_____

_____

_____

_____

_____

_____

_____

Why Do Kids with ADHD Struggle to Ask for Help?

We have already established that asking for help is difficult for many students with ADHD. In fact, some of you can attest to this based on your own personal experiences. The question that begs to be answered is why? As the expert of yourself, see if any of these explanations resonate with you.

Fear of Judgment or Rejection: By now, it should be pretty clear that students who have ADHD face judgment regularly. I would say that half of my clients worry about being perceived as "different." They reject the diagnosis they have been assigned; they refuse to take advantage of academic accommodations, despite knowing how valuable they will be to their academic and personal success.

When all is said and done, they don't want any possibility of being viewed as incapable. Add to this the layers of judgment they face regularly, and it makes sense why these students are so keenly aware of what it means to be judged as less-than.

When they are late for class, their teachers can't help but pass judgment. How difficult can it be to get yourself to class on time or to hand in assignments when they are due? (Anyone who has experienced life with ADHD knows the answer to this question.)

Friends and classmates snicker and heave sighs of frustration when the kid surrenders to his impulsivity and calls out in class, not once, but multiple times a day. Parents throw their hands up in frustration when their kid comes home with the second behavior notice of the week, and it's only Tuesday.

So often, students with ADHD are misunderstood. They're viewed as defiant, incompetent, and inadequate, and this just is not the case. Given these circumstances, how can a student experience anything other than tremendous fear that their requests for help won't be greeted with open arms? This genuine fear of additional ridicule creates an understandable reluctance to ask for help.

I can feel you nodding your head; some of you may have tears welling in your eyes because you live this every day. You don't want to be perceived as weak or incompetent—this will only compound the shame and embarrassment you're already feeling, right? I get it because I see this with my clients all the time. They know they need the help, but they will do anything to prevent getting additional negative attention.

Difficulty Recognizing the Need for Help: How does a kid not know when she needs help? Isn't it obvious? Her ship is sinking—the deck furniture is sliding to the starboard side of the vessel, and she needs to act fast. Her friends see it; her teachers see it, but she can't. Here's why:

Impaired Executive Functioning: ADHD is associated with difficulties in executive functioning, which include skills like organization, planning, and self-monitoring. These executive function deficits can make it challenging for students with ADHD to recognize when they are struggling or falling behind in their tasks. They may have difficulty assessing their own performance objectively and identifying the need for help or intervention.

Inconsistent Attention and Focus: One of the core symptoms of ADHD is inattention. Students who have ADHD may struggle to sustain attention to tasks, leading to missed instructions, important details, or cues that they need help. This inconsistency in attention can make it difficult for them to recognize when they are about to veer off course, as they may have gaps in their awareness due to distractibility.

Difficulty with Self-Reflection: ADHD can affect a student's ability to reflect on his own behaviors and thoughts. He may have difficulty recognizing his own patterns of struggle or identifying the underlying causes of his difficulties. This lack of self-reflection can hinder his ability to realize when he needs help.

Impulsivity and Lack of Patience: Impulsivity is a common trait in ADHD, which can result in children impulsively jumping into tasks without considering the need for assistance.

I often use this analogy when discussing the idea of thinking things through before acting: Let's say you are planning to take a cross-country trip in your car from Philadelphia to Los Angeles. Would you just hop in your car and go? Anyone who is banking on a smooth adventure recognizes the importance of one key step—planning.

First, you'll have to plan your route. Are you taking the northern or southern roads? You need to pack food and beverages—a hungry and thirsty driver is a distracted, impatient, and easily frustrated driver! Who is going with you? What season is it, and what clothing should you pack? How long will the ride take? Are you stopping along the way? (I hope so. How can you drive across our beautiful country and not see all it offers?)

The same theory applies to an assignment. You can't just dive head-first into a task without following some basic preliminary steps:

✓ What are the directions?
✓ When is it due?

✓ Are there aspects of this assignment that you do not understand and may need to ask for help?
✓ What does "DONE" look like?
✓ How do you need to submit it?

A kid who has ADHD frequently jumps into a situation without thinking things through. The fact that they struggle with patience makes it challenging for kids to wait for help or seek it out proactively.

STOP and think: What prevents you from asking for help?

_____
_____
_____
_____
_____
_____
_____
_____
_____
_____
_____

Why Asking for Help is Critical to Your Success

Understanding why students with ADHD are reluctant to ask for help, it's incumbent upon us to discuss why it's so important for you to navigate your discomfort and advocate for yourself. I'm not saying that choosing _not_ to self-advocate will doom you to epic failure and emotional torment, but I suggest this: If you can process your feelings about asking for help and then create a game plan to address your concerns, you're likely to obtain assistance that will empower you and help you achieve your goals. Consider the following scenarios and see if any of them speak to you.

Academic Struggles: Without seeking help, a student may struggle to keep up with academic demands. ADHD can affect attention, organization, and time management, making it challenging to complete assignments, stay focused in class, and effectively study for exams. As a result, grades and overall academic performance may suffer.

Emotional and Psychological Impact: The price for not seeking help frequently impacts students' social and emotional well-being. "Staci" is a fifteen-year-old student of mine, and when she worked with me, she was emotionally vulnerable. She was riddled with debilitating anxiety in her academic performance: The school day was a total loss as she frequently sat in class, unable to focus on lectures and directions because all she could hear was the deafening volume of her anxiety barking in her brain. "Don't be late; don't be late; don't be late. Pay attention today. You have to pay attention, or you're going to fail the next assignment like you did last time. Forget it. You're going to fail no matter what you do."

When she arrived home, her anxiety was so overwhelming that she could not initiate her work. Battles between her and her parents were a nightly occurrence, and there were not enough boxes of tissues to wipe away her tears of shame and frustration.

As we worked together, we unpacked Staci's resistance. It turns out Staci was too embarrassed to ask for help. She knew she was smart—she was in all honors and AP classes. But sometimes, she didn't even know what she didn't know. She didn't always recognize when she needed help, nor could she determine how to articulate her message to her teachers or parents.

After processing these issues, we devised a plan of action that felt comfortable to her, and Staci slowly but surely met with her teachers and got the help she needed. Consequently, her anxiety levels decreased, and she felt much more relaxed when she was engaged in her academics.

Social Consequences: When students don't seek help, they can experience serious social consequences. "Jasper" was a middle-school student I worked with, starting when he was in the sixth grade. Diagnosed with ADHD in second grade, Jasper's impulsivity had gotten him into hot water with his peers and adults alike. He struggled to establish friendships, and those he did successfully woo into friendships were short-lived because his behavior was so frustrating.

When he and his friends stood together in a group to talk, Jasper would inevitably interrupt someone. Playdates would end in shouting matches because he would break off into what his friends called his "own orbit," unaware that the baseball game or video game was still going on. Ultimately, his veering off course would lead to his team or partner's loss, and all fingers would point to Jasper.

By the time Jasper came to my office, he was struggling mightily. Academically, his teachers had lost their patience, and his behavior had exacted such a huge toll on his peers that they no longer sought him out, instead resorting to nasty taunts and bullying.

This kid was defeated. But with the introduction of some strategies that taught him self-awareness, social skills, and executive functioning skills for school, along with the addition of a low-dose stimulant medication, this kid did a 180-degree turnaround. By the end of the school year, Jasper was a regular leader in class discussions, successfully managing to stay on track. He had one best friend and was slowly developing relationships with acquaintances in his grade.

Missed Opportunities for Support: When students do not advocate for themselves, they can miss out on receiving the support required to succeed and that which they have the *right* to receive. "Hillary" was a student I worked with while she was in high school. An extremely proud young woman, Hillary took great pains to make sure she did everything on her own. This approach worked pretty well until she started taking AP courses her sophomore year, and then things took a nosedive. She couldn't keep up with the volume of reading in her APUSH class, and her previously effective note-taking skills weren't enough to get the job done for this class. Working with online resources was not enough to figure out how to find the log of thirty-two to the base of four in her math class. She was tanking—and fast.

Up to this point in her career, Hillary had refused all formal accommodations outlined in her IEP, claiming she didn't want to be different from her peers or seen as incapable. With her ship taking on water faster than she could scoop it overboard, she sat with me and wept.

I gently broached the topic of reexamining her situation through a different lens. Using diabetes as an analogy for her situation, I asked her whether it would be special treatment or cheating others of opportunity if a diabetic used insulin to keep his blood sugar under control. She sat up and looked at me, her eyes wide. I went on to ask a similar question about a student who needed glasses to read or an injured friend who needed to use crutches until her leg healed from her surgery.

Hillary laughed because she knew exactly where I was going with all of this: All of us have areas where we need extra support. No one gets off scot-free. At that moment, her academic "diabetes" was out of control, and the situation was taking a huge toll on her, emotionally and academically. We reviewed the accommodations in her IEP and identified those she felt most comfortable starting with. Then, we built on from there.

By the middle of her sophomore year, Hillary was meeting regularly with her teachers and had started to use teacher-issued notes along with an eBook for her APUSH textbook, and she was rocking it!

Strategies

"Okay, Coach, okay! I get it; it's important to ask for help. Now what?" Now, my feisty student, it's time to get our hands dirty with the strategies that will help you advocate for yourself.

Basics

Let's begin with the basics. Just as you might address the who, what, where, when, and how in an essay, there are some fundamental components you need to be aware of if you are going to get the help you seek:

Recognize when you need help. The first step is to create a sense of self-awareness. Your mind and body communicate with you regularly. Think about it: Your stomach growls when you are hungry; your body increases its temperature when you have an infection; your head may ache when you are feeling stressed. You get signals when your schoolwork requires extra help. Think back on the most recent time when you needed assistance. What were your "tells"?

Feeling stuck: This feeling often settles in when you don't know how to initiate an assignment. You know what the finished product should look like, but getting from point A to point B is hard to envision.

Resisting work altogether: Most of us would agree that the least desirable and most difficult tasks are those we try to avoid. Doesn't it make sense that when you are attempting something that makes little sense, you might avoid it completely?

Constantly weighing on your mind: This is your brain telling you that you feel unsure. Assignments that we are unsure about tend to follow us until we get relief in the form of help from others.

Experiencing physical symptoms: If you have an assignment and it's causing you an upset stomach, vomiting, dizziness, headaches, or the jitters, this is a pretty good indication that help is required.

Having anxiety: Feeling overwhelmed about an assignment is also a clear sign you should ask for help.

What is the help or information you are seeking? Once you recognize the signs of needing help, you can move on to the next step, which is determining the help you need. Look at the assignment. Is it a math concept that doesn't make sense to you? Is the prompt you received for the history essay too vague, and you need more structure? Are you unsure about the formatting of your science lab? Are you confused about due dates? Once you can discern *what* you are looking for, you can decide what to do next.

Who might be able to help you? This step is not necessarily just about subject-specific help. That is helpful indeed. However, maybe there is a specific teacher or professor within that department who can better address your question. Take the example of the science lab: the professor may be great at answering questions about the content of the course, but his graduate assistant may be in a better position to advise you about the formatting of the lab report because she has experience working with the software you used.

How should you seek that help? Some students don't mind walking right up to the instructor and requesting help, while others bristle at the idea of being so bold. Maybe an email is more comfortable, as it will give you time to digest the instructor's reply. Similarly, a text might feel equally comfortable as long as the teacher or instructor gives you permission to do so. A note on a teacher or professor's desks or, for younger students, a call from a parent is an effective means of reaching out for help. Regardless of the chosen method of communication, be sure to list all your questions and concerns before meeting with your instructor to ensure you address everything on your mind.

When and where can you meet with this person? Are you someone who doesn't mind meeting in a public arena, like a Lunch and Learn session, or do you prefer something more private, like meeting before class or during office hours?

How to know whether you got the help you need? So, you asked for help, took the next step, and met with the person you felt could best help you. Good job! You'll know you received the proper help if you can explain the content back to the teacher accurately in your own words. You may want to ask the individual helping you if he or she would mind if you recorded your meeting so you can reference it in the future when you are working on your own. Alternatively, take notes so you have something to help refresh your mind when you get home. If you have follow-up questions after you meet, that's okay. Reach out and request another meeting.

Put it to the test. Go home and work on it while the conversation is fresh in your mind. Review your notes or the recording you made.

Attempt the assignment on your own; if all goes well, you're golden. If not, track what makes sense and what doesn't, and then return for additional support.

STOP and think: Which of these strategies (You can choose more than one!) seems helpful and user-friendly to you?

_____

_____

_____

_____

_____

_____

_____

_____

_____

_____

STOP and think: How will you put them to the test?

_____

_____

_____

_____

_____

_____

_____

_____

_____

_____

_____

NOTE TO SELF:

"What if I don't know what I don't know?" I can't tell you the number of times a student has asked me this question. They know they don't understand something, but they just can't seem to pinpoint the issue.

As I have discussed with each of my students, it's okay to say exactly _that_ when meeting with your teacher. Start with what you _do_ know and what _does_ make sense. As you get further into the conversation, one of two things will happen.

First, you may get clarity about what was confusing, and second, you may also start to actually understand the very thing that was confusing to begin with. It's totally okay not to understand exactly what is eluding you. Talking it through with someone who can help you with the content can help in solving that mystery.

Build Your Self-Confidence

Be Your Own Little Red Engine: Once you have addressed the basics, it's time to switch gears and start building your self-confidence. Remember the Little Red Engine? He faced certain difficulties as he struggled to pull a heavy load up a mountainous railroad. All the while, he pulled and chugged, saying, "I think I can. I think I can." This mantra stoked his confidence and his belief in himself to accomplish this noble mission ahead of him.

You can achieve the same goal by following his example. Use positive self-talk to get you through the tough times, and don't forget to praise yourself when you meet with success! As a distance runner, I have frequently used my sport as an analogy for academic success. In addition to proper training, the secret to completing a long-distance run is literally taking it one mile at a time. The same is true with academics—take it one paragraph, one paper, one exam at a time. "One mile at a time...." is my mantra. What is yours?

STOP and think: What is your personal mantra, and why does it inspire you?

_____

_____

_____

_____

_____

_____

_____

_____

_____

_____

_____

Recognize Your Own Strengths

You have them. Because of or despite ADHD, you bring a lot to the table. Maybe you have learned how to capitalize on your penchant for hyper-focusing on something that interests you.

Problem-solving might be easier for you because you can think out-of-the-box. Your social skills may help you facilitate relationships with peers and teachers in such a way that they will help you when you need it most.

Perhaps you are a singer, actor, athlete, artist, scientist, debater…. whatever you are, you are incredible, and you have so much to offer yourself and others. Use your well-established strengths to build toward new success stories.

Look at Your Track Record

You are still here despite any challenges you may have had up to this point. This suggests you have met with varying degrees of success. Picture yourself climbing up a steep mountain. If you look ahead of you, all you can see is rocky terrain, enticing you with its beauty and wonder to continue your upward trajectory. However, what's incredibly important is to admire the view below you. Look at the base of the mountain and acknowledge how far you have climbed! Take in those sharp rocks and steep drop-offs that you managed to navigate. You got yourself to this checkpoint in your hike. So many people forget to take time for this critical point of validation.

Think about this: What steps did you take? Who did you turn to for help? How did you sustain that momentum? You did not start off as an "expert" when you started this journey. No one does. But you tapped into your resources, and you got yourself this far. Continue to use these strategies and forge ahead!

Be Realistic with Your Expectations

We are all guilty of setting the bar high in our expectations for ourselves. "When I get home, I'll have a snack, and then I will write my history paper, study for math, write my lab report, and walk the dog before Mom starts dinner." Umm, I admire the tenacity, but you and I both know these goals cannot be met within the approximately two-hour time period we are talking about, right?

Personal goals and expectations are important; they help to guide our productivity and inform our sense of accomplishment. *Do* set the bar for yourself, but make sure the standards you seek to meet are realistic and not ideal. Let's take the example we just read about and make a realistic set of expectations for the night.

- Come home and eat a snack.
- Create an outline for the history paper and write the thesis statement (Tomorrow, I will write the introductory paragraph and topic sentences for each section).
- Review for math test (It's in two days, so I will complete the chapter review today, and tomorrow, I'll practice problems I missed in that review).
- Eat dinner, then walk the dog.
- If there is extra time remaining, I'll finish the first section of my lab report—it's not due for five more days.

By creating a realistic set of expectations, you set yourself up for success, boosting your self-confidence. These victories will inspire your momentum and future victory!

GOAL

Goal: Identify at least two strategies you can use to help you get the help you need and create a plan of action for their use.

_____

_____

_____

_____

_____

_____

_____

_____

_____

_____

Asking for help is not always easy; for many students, whether they have ADHD or not, it can feel like a daunting venture. It's important to remember that self-advocacy is a sign of strength. By engaging with others to get the assistance you need, you open so many doors, including increased productivity, development of personal and academic skill sets, autonomy, and an increase in self-esteem. Failure to self-advocate can lead to academic struggles that cause lower grades and falling behind in assignments, solidifying an already-well established sense of insecurity and failure.

Remember, you possess so many wonderful strengths and talents as is evidenced by your standing here today. Stay strong, believe in yourself, and never hesitate to ask for help when you need it. You deserve support, understanding, and success.

Key Takeaways: Chapter 5

- ✓ **Seeking help is often difficult** for a lot of reasons: fear of rejection or judgment, difficulty recognizing when assistance is needed, impulsivity, and lack of patience. As a result, many students will not pursue the assistance they need, leading to increased stress and anxiety.

- ✓ **Asking for help is critical** to personal and academic success, as not doing so can make life more difficult. Specifically, failure to self-advocate can lead to increased academic struggles, which can result in lower grades and falling behind in their coursework. These students can also experience increased emotional and psychological duress, leading to feelings of helplessness and resignation. A student's struggles can also extend to social consequences as their peers may isolate this impulsive and unreliable classmate. Finally, failure to ask for help can cause missed opportunities to receive assistance they legally and ethically have the right to access, including formal accommodations provided by an IEP or 504 agreement.

- ✓ **Utilizing key strategies** will enable a student to feel more comfortable and confident about asking for help. It's important to start with the basics, which include self-awareness and the recognition that help is in order; knowing what and who to ask; how to access that individual; preparing for the conversation ahead of time; and knowing how to determine whether the help the student received was effective.

✓ **Additional strategies** include building self-confidence, being cognizant of one's own strengths, examining one's track record, and setting realistic expectations and goals. These collective strategies can contribute to a student's sense of self-efficacy and confidence when seeking help.

✓ **By not asking for help,** students with ADHD may face academic struggles, resulting in lower grades and falling behind in their coursework. The emotional and psychological impact can be significant, leading to increased stress, anxiety, and feelings of failure. Additionally, the social consequences of not seeking help may lead to strained relationships, isolation, and a negative self-image.

Chapter 6
The Parent-Student Dynamic Duo:
Trust, Triumph, and Lots of Patience!

One of the greatest challenges my students and their families face is the relationship they share with one another. Students want to be seen as independent people, capable of making decisions and forging the life they choose to lead.

Parents and guardians naturally worry about their kids—they want to make sure they are healthy, successful, safe, and happy. Even as their children get older and mature, it can be difficult for parents to let go and have faith in their children's ability to live independent, successful lives.

Managing Relationships

Living with ADHD can add complications to the home environment. From students' perspectives, they feel discouraged, overwhelmed, defeated, and ashamed. They believe they are capable of success, but their inattention, disorganization, and chronic tardiness, among other challenges, make success elusive. Try as they might, they just can't get the ball rolling and sustain the momentum.

As if their own self-imposed pressure and sense of failure isn't enough, they have their parents and guardians to contend with. So many of my students voice their frustration about their helicopter parents who constantly hover, managing their time, assignments, and appointments with teachers. If it's really intense, the Blackhawk helicopter parents not only take over the student's academic arena, but they insert themselves in the social and extra-curricular terrain as well. They don't just hover; they land squarely on their kids' heads. It's overwhelming and unnecessary, and it drives my students crazy. However, after patiently listening to and validating my clients' state of exasperation, I invite them to look at their parents' experiences. These are some issues that fuel parental helicopters:

Concern for Academic Success: Parents and guardians naturally want to see their children meet with academic success, which makes sense. Education is one of the best predictors of finding a job and being successful at it. When their kid struggles with organizational skills, completion of homework, test taking, time management, and self-advocacy (among other important skills), parents become concerned about their child's academic success, and they also worry about the potential long-term implications their child will face because of these difficulties.

Social and Behavioral Challenges: No one wants their child to be viewed as "different" from the other kids in school. Being a kid is tough enough without adding any labels that might indicate a child is anything other than "normal." But ADHD brings some zest to a child.

As we have discussed in previous chapters, they process information differently; they view the world uniquely; they often think creatively, and many students who struggle with attention frequently visit what feels like, to others, another orbit. All of this is to say there is nothing wrong with any of these characteristics or experiences; it just adds extra color and spice—and sometimes the consequence is social isolation and rejection.

ADHD can impact a child's ability to navigate socially, which may affect skills like following rules, reading social cues correctly, and self-control. Consequently, parents worry about their kid's ability to establish and sustain friendships or engage in appropriate classroom behavior.

Misconceptions and Stigma: Parents and guardians can become concerned about misconceptions and stigmas related to ADHD. Sometimes, people think kids with ADHD are defiant, intellectually delayed, and downright rude. Given these misconceptions of ADHD, it's understandable why parents of these kids are so concerned about the potential negative impact these misinformed people will have on their child's self-esteem and overall well-being.

Managing Day-to-Day Challenges: As we have already covered in great detail, having ADHD means constantly facing challenges in daily life. Establishing and perpetuating routines and controlling one's impulsivity are only two areas in which a child faces consistent difficulty. At some point, parents may experience an increase in stress and frustration while trying to help their child weigh and balance these demands. In turn, this state of emotional turmoil can negatively impact their relationship with their child.

Uncertainty About Treatment and Support: Sometimes, wading through school and professional resources is overwhelming. So much information comes down the pipeline that parents don't know where to begin. Do they start with medication? They've heard stimulant medications can have negative side effects, including tics and appetite suppression, so how can that possibly be beneficial, even if it means their kid will pay attention in class? They've been told to enlist in the services of a therapist to help their child process all their emotions related to their ADHD, but that won't necessarily give their child the skills he needs to overcome his academic and social challenges. Someone told them to find an academic coach, but should they do that before the medication or after? The myriad of intervention treatments and conflicting advice is enough for even the calmest of minds to erupt.

STOP and Think: Did you realize how much your ADHD could impact your family?

_____

_____

_____

_____

_____

_____

_____

_____

_____

_____

_____

Having this brief glimpse into your parents' perspective, isn't their frustration and stress more understandable now? Don't get me wrong: I am not justifying their aggression or frustration, but I am giving you a different lens through which to view your parents and how ADHD affects _them_. Remember, this neurological disability is not just impacting you; it's affecting your caretakers as well.

With these concerns and tensions forming the foundation of the family dynamic, it's not surprising that sparks fly when the two parties come together. Mom nags the student with her litany of 'Did yous'— Did you remember to clean your room? Did you talk with your teacher about your late assignment? Did you meet with your guidance counselor? Did you do your homework, and did you submit it online?

The list goes on and on. In response to these seemingly non-stop inquiries, the kid pushes back. She tells Mom to back off. She says she handed in the assignment, but the truth is, she _did_ forget about it, and now it's two days late. She avoids her parents altogether because that's the only recourse she has to shield herself from the onslaught of daily inquisitions. Her withdrawal prompts even more parental involvement. The fighting begins, the tears flow, and the doors slam shut.

This scenario plays out in houses across the country, and it takes a tremendous toll on students and parents alike.

STOP and Think: What do your parents do that is counterproductive?

_____
_____
_____
_____
_____
_____
_____
_____
_____
_____
_____
_____

STOP and Think: Can you think of some suggestions you might give them that would actually help you?

_____

_____

_____

_____

_____

_____

_____

_____

_____

_____

So, How Do We Stop the Madness?

Let's acknowledge something many parents struggle to admit: they are not perfect. They are humans, complete with blemishes and scars that tell the stories of their own frequently flawed attempts to establish themselves as autonomous people.

If we are going to be honest, this struggle is very much a part of the human condition. Every person is just trying to figure out who they are and where they fit into this world. But I digress. My point is that your very human parents are *not* perfect. Yes, I just said it, and I will say it again. Parents are NOT perfect. Many of us like to think we are, but the reality is—get ready for this, kids—we make mistakes. Gasp! It's true! You kids didn't come with manuals, so your parents and guardians are learning, much like a student progresses through his classes, trying to learn, grow, and succeed.

The only difference is, students have access to guidance in the form of help from teachers, professors, study guides, online resources, and notes from older classmates. Parents, on the other hand, often have few road maps, guidebooks, or official resources to help us navigate the privilege of being your parents. I frequently joke that if you *did* come with a manual, it's likely the doctors threw it out with the placenta! Eww, I know.

STOP and Think: How does it feel to hear someone say parents aren't perfect?

_____

_____

_____

_____

_____

_____

_____

_____

_____

_____

Don't panic, and don't put this book down. I hear your wheels turning... you think this chapter is going to be dedicated to defending your parents and guardians, right? You're waiting for me to say you should respect these adults in your life because, after all, they are raising you, and you have to give them your respect.

Nope. I'm not about to make a federal court case to persuade you of any such thing. As a matter of fact, you may even be surprised to hear me say respect has to be earned. Just because your guardians and parents are playing this role in your life doesn't automatically mean you have to respect them. They need to act in a way that deserves such reverence.

How do they achieve this? They speak to you respectfully and don't resort to name calling or making wild accusations. They inquire about your feelings and opinions. They make time for you and are there for the times you need them—and the times you don't. But that respect runs both ways. You are held to the same standard of behavior. So many of my students want a sense of agency in their lives. They want their voices to be heard and their opinions to matter to the parents, guardians, teachers, and coaches they interface with regularly. Sadly, for many, this doesn't happen often enough, if ever at all. But if you really want this level of recognition and respect, you must offer these adults the same.

STOP and Think: What do your parents do to show you respect?

_____

_____

_____

_____

_____

_____

_____

_____

_____

_____

STOP and Think: What do you do to show your parents respect?

_____

_____

_____

_____

_____

_____

_____

_____

_____

_____

_____

So why am I taking the time to include a chapter about you and your parents and guardians? For most of you, these people are the most influential human beings you will ever have in your life. It's not just about the necessities they provide you; it's about the lessons and values they instill in you and the unconditional love they provide so that you can grow and evolve into self-assured, healthy, productive people, able to make valuable contributions to the world around you.

For most of you, these are the people you live with, so it's reasonable to assume you spend a fair amount of time with them. Home needs to be a place where everyone feels safe. Too often, one of the top reasons families enlist in my services is because the family unit is in crisis, and no one feels emotionally safe. ADHD can do that.

This chapter is about giving you and the adults in your life the opportunity to bring peace back to your lives, to stop the fighting (or at least decrease it significantly), and to enable you to appreciate and respect one another. After delving into this chapter, I hope you will identify some strategies to facilitate a healthy and mutually respectful relationship with your parents and guardians. Read on.

As is true for society at large, having some rules in place helps to bring order to the home and levels the playing field for all parties. Let's lay out the rules for a healthy and respectful parent/child relationship.

Agree: It's important that, from the outset, everyone understands they are on the same team. You may not agree on all or anything, but when all is said and done, you are all working toward helping you to feel confident and successful.

Calm: It's so important for everyone to stay as calm, cool, and collected as possible. Cooler heads can hear what's being said. Remaining calm is critical to accurately pinpointing the issues and identifying feasible solutions that everyone can live with. If any participant feels overwhelmed, it is incumbent for the parties to recognize this and take a break. Some families find it helpful to have a keyword to let each other know when they need to pause. Words like "time out" and "walk away" have been used. Recognizing the power of humor, my clients and I have identified silly words like "watermelon," "pickle juice," and "cafe' ole'" to break the tension.

No Phones or Devices: Very little can be accomplished when phones are present during a conversation. Vibrations, beeps, rings, boops, and flashing lights all interfere with the ability to concentrate and focus on the topic at hand. Additionally, it's rude to use these devices when you are engaged in conversation with others. Make eye contact, listen actively, and leave your phones and other devices outside of the room.

Privacy: There is nothing more humiliating to a kid than being called out in front of her siblings. Brothers and sisters are intuitive: even if they don't know the specifics of the situation, they are keenly aware their sibling is in trouble or having a problem. They have been privy to the fighting and the late-night conversations about missed assignments. Hold your conversation with your parents in a private part of the house. Your business is nobody else's business, period.

Respect: I hinted at this earlier in the chapter. Use respectful language. Avoid name-calling and insults. Screaming and yelling will get you nowhere. You have a valid message, but you lose your audience the second you shout. If you get angry or frustrated—and that will happen—take a step back, breathe, collect your thoughts, and try again. Walk away, if necessary, but when you come back, you are perfectly within your right to tell your parent or guardian how you are feeling and why.

NOTE ON PHYSICAL AND EMOTIONAL ABUSE:

There is no place for abuse in a family home. Tempers will flare, and people will get frustrated and exasperated, but whether it's a parent or a child, there is no justification for abuse of any kind. If you feel unsafe going into these types of conversations, it may be time to bring in a neutral third party—a family member, family friend, guidance counselor, therapist, clergy member, or another trusted adult.

Respect Family Togetherness and Bedtime: Certain times and circumstances need to be cordoned off from stressful conversations. Being hit in the face with inquiries about school first thing in the morning or right when you walk in the door is unsettling for the individual at the receiving end of the inquisition. It's better if parents wait until a period of time has passed so their students can wake up or relax enough to get their bearings and participate meaningfully.

Mealtimes are meant to be relaxing, when families can come together to talk about their day, crack some jokes, and just enjoy being with one another. It's definitely not the time to broach potentially heated topics. Finally, bedtime is a big no-no. Your parents are tired; you are tired. Nothing good is going to come from talking about trouble right before bed. Any potentially stressful conversations need to stop at least two hours before bedtime to increase the likelihood of good sleep. Tomorrow is another day.

Let Others Finish their Sentence: I know, I know, this is not an easy feat. Dad says something inaccurate or misguided, or maybe he's right and you just don't want to admit it. Either way, you must let your parents finish their sentences, and they must do the same for you. This gives everyone a chance to speak and have their voices heard.

STOP and Think: Are there any rules you feel I missed? If so, what would you add to the list?

Strategies

Review the Rules: Before each meeting, review the rules we just outlined and make sure everyone feels comfortable with and capable of following them. Add additional rules as needed.

Create an Agenda: Before you sit down with your parent or guardian, you and they need to have in mind what you hope to gain from the impending conversation. What are your concerns, and what are theirs? What have you tried so far to help yourself? Where have you met with success, and where do you still need support? Sometimes, writing these thoughts down helps to keep the conversation on track and assists with accountability. It may be helpful for both parties to share their agendas with one another ahead of time.

Use "I" Messages: Speaking for yourself tends to prevent accusations and messages of blame from flying, while decreasing defensiveness. They allow the speaker to own their feelings without blaming the other party, preventing the listener from feeling the need to defend themselves or shut down to protect themselves.

In Times of Uncertainty, Ask: If someone says something that doesn't make sense, ask them to restate it in a way that you can understand. Make no assumptions! We all know the saying about the verb 'assume'. "It makes an ass out of u and me." If your mom says something hurtful to you, tell her what you heard and ask her if that's what she meant to say. She may not realize that her words were hurtful.

Check in Regularly: No matter how old you are, it's important for you to be proactive with your communication. By now, you know your parents are sitting on the edge of their seats every day, waiting for the other shoe to drop about this assignment or that exam or this behavior report. Do you have an update on these topics of conversation? Let them know. It will decrease their angst, which means they will be calmer, and you won't be so aggravated!

Initiate Communication: I know what many of you will think when I explain this next suggestion: Why is it up to me to communicate with them? I'll tell you why, kiddo. Imagine a night when your parent or guardian is all up in your business, nagging you left and right about what you have for homework tonight—when it's due, how long it will take you, and whether you submitted it. My blood pressure is rising just thinking about this scene! On the other hand, picture yourself letting your parents know about your homework—your plan to complete it and that you successfully submitted it. Imagine the amazement on their faces when they get this report at the end of each night! Your actions, your choice. Which one can you live with?

Establish Healthy Boundaries: Under the best of circumstances, parents can struggle with this concept. Most will want to encourage your independence as you grow up, but it's only natural that they will have some bumps along the way. It's exciting and difficult to watch you guys get older! In these initial meetings, discuss each party's responsibilities. For students, your job is to go to school (regularly and on time), learn, play, or hang out with your friends, study and complete your assignments, and take care of your emotional and physical well-being. Aside from the basics of providing a roof over your head, food, and clothing, parents need to ensure you are physically and emotionally safe. For kids who have ADHD, part of that safety includes getting the support you need to succeed.

For each kid, that looks a little different. I have some students who find it helpful to have company or body doubling while they are working, but that's it—they don't want help with the initiation or completion of homework. They take comfort in just knowing someone is physically in the same room as them. Other kids want a more hands-on approach—they want someone to read over their paper and make some editing suggestions, or they want to review math facts the night before their exam. Every kid is different, and it's incumbent upon you and your parents to reach a mutually agreeable compromise. At the end of the day, the goal is to promote your sense of autonomy while providing the support you may need.

Collaboratively Problem-Solve: When parents and their kids work together to solve an issue, the process is more peaceful and productive for both parties. As we have discussed, the first step is agreeing to be respectful toward one another. The next step is to establish goals you both can agree on, making sure that these goals are realistic and within reach.

Engaging in a shared goal-setting process ensures both parties are equally invested, and that mutual trust is at play between the parties. You, the student, need to have agency in the decision-making process. What strategies will be used? With whom will you (and your family) consult? When will meetings take place with the professional? (This is especially important for older students who have extra-curricular obligations they need to fulfill.) Your involvement will empower you, leaving you with a strong sense of self-confidence, perhaps for the first time ever!

Next, you can brainstorm strategies, agreeing to be equally open to creative ideas. Once you implement the game plan, it's important to regroup and evaluate the plan, paying attention to what worked and what still needs to be addressed.

Using some or all these strategies will help to bridge the distance that may have developed as a result of your struggles with ADHD. Together, you and your parents and guardians can work as a team, building trust and respect for one another. Will you become the best of friends? Not necessarily, and that's okay. But with a newfound understanding of each other and the situation at play with your ADHD, hopefully, a level of peace can enter your home, reducing the stress for everyone and making your living space a place where everyone feels safer and more understood.

GOAL

Goal: Identify three strategies you feel will be helpful. Describe how you plan to use them.

_____

_____

_____

_____

_____

_____

_____

_____

_____

_____

So many of my students voice their frustration about having so many adults controlling their lives. They just want a sense of independence; they long to have a voice, to have their goals, dreams, and aspirations respected. They do not want to be talked down to; they are insulted and frequently humiliated when this happens. I agree with you.

As I have said to so many of my students, you are an untapped resource. Your undeniable gift of looking at a problem through a unique lens and coming up with any number of viable solutions is incredible. Who cares if it's unconventional? Does it matter that no one else has attempted it in the manner you are proposing?

Yes, sometimes you need to follow guidelines, like when you are writing a lab report or solving long division, but there are plenty of other situations that lend themselves to creativity and innovation. I'll be the first to admit that many adults need to do a better job of not only listening to but respecting you. That can start here with this chapter. Use it as a road map; feel free to make changes as you see fit.

Key Takeaways: Chapter 6

- ✓ **ADHD impacts students and their parents** in ways that differ from one another.
- ✓ **Parental concerns about their children who have ADHD** include concerns about academic success, social and behavioral challenges, misconceptions and stigmas about ADHD, management of daily tasks, and uncertainty about treatment and support options. These concerns can cause stress and anxiety, which can cause parents to become overly involved in their children's academic performance.
- ✓ **Establishing ground rules is a critical component** of creating a sound foundation for the parent-child relationship. These rules include being respectful, allowing one another to complete sentences, ensuring conversations take place privately away from other relatives in the home, eliminating devices during conversations, and avoiding abusive behavior.
- ✓ **All students need to have a sense of agency** when it comes to decision-making.
- ✓ **Effective strategies that parents and children can use** include reviewing the rules, creating an agenda for each conversation, using "I" messages, asking for clarification when warranted, having regular check-ins, establishing healthy boundaries, creating student-initiated communication about assignments and plans of action, and establishing parent-student collaborative problem-solving.

Chapter 7
From FOMO to Focus: Finding Balance in the Social Media Sphere

There has been an elephant sitting in each of our homes for several years, yet no one has addressed or tamed it. Social media has a far-reaching presence in our society and daily living habits. It sneaks into children's bedrooms, sometimes at all hours of the night. It disrupts even the simplest of communication between children and parents because it is so enticing and too difficult to resist. It sabotages academic momentum and success, and it poisons interpersonal relationships. And yet, it is equally beneficial, as it brings people together, enabling us to overcome the separation of hundreds, sometimes thousands of miles between us.

As the COVID-19 pandemic demonstrated, in many ways, social media offered a resuscitative lifeline to hundreds of thousands of people when we could not interact with others in person. People who share common passions and interests bond because of this powerful beast, and those belonging to traditionally marginalized populations, like those related to race, culture, religion, and sexual and gender minorities, find strength through the connections and relationships they forge—relationships they may have otherwise struggled to find in the in-person world. And therein lies the difficulty. Social media is a powerful tool for all of us, but this is particularly true for children, whose developing brains are vulnerable to the power of this world of communication.

Managing Social Media

On May 23, 2023, Surgeon General Dr. Vivek Murthy released an advisory about the negative impact social media has on the mental health of youth. While acknowledging the benefits of this communication tool, Dr. Murthy leaves little doubt about the dangerous effects on children's emotional wellbeing, going so far as to state, "There is growing evidence to suggest that social media use may harm the developing brains of children... potential health effects include increased symptoms of depression, anxiety, ADHD, self-harm, and eating disorders.[11]"

---

[11] U.S. Department of Health and Human Services, "Surgeon General Issues New Advisory About Effects Social Media Use Has on Youth Mental Health," May 23, 2023, https://www.hhs.gov/about/news/2023/05/23/surgeon-general-issues-new-advisory-about-effects-social-media-use-has-youth-mental-health.html.

Finding a balance that gives our children access to exciting worlds of appropriate information, social interaction, and discovery—while using common sense guidelines to keep them safe—is key to ensuring their physical and emotional well-being at all ages.

In this chapter, I openly and willingly acknowledge the many benefits associated with social media. Even students who have ADHD can use this powerful tool to assist with establishing time management, limiting distractions, tracking assignment progress, and meeting deadlines. On the flip side, social media can become the bane of a student's existence, especially when that student is grappling with the impact of ADHD.

Sometimes, this digital advancement is detrimental to the ADHD mind, undercutting an individual's ability to establish and maintain independence. Social media is not going anywhere; it has become an integral part of human communication and society. Having said that, I will delve into these challenges and suggest some practical strategies to help you strike a balance between social media engagement and fulfilling your "real-life" obligations, including having fun offline!

As is true with using any powerful tool, when it comes to using social media, you must recognize the signs of trouble. This section of the chapter will empower you to recognize when social media is becoming a disruption to your emotional, social, and academic wellbeing.

Finally, this chapter will conclude with some suggestions for useful apps you can use to assist you with organizational and time management skills, as well as apps that can promote healthy well-being.

Social media serves as an amazing platform that enriches our lives in so many ways. But as a consumer, especially one who has ADHD, you need to understand the advantages and the potentially detrimental impact it can have on your life.

Hannah Bookbinder

STOP and Think: What do you use social media for? Socializing? Games? Relaxation?

_____
_____
_____
_____
_____
_____
_____
_____
_____
_____

STOP and Think: Do you ever find that your use of social media prevents you from getting work done or socializing with others?

_____

_____

_____

_____

_____

_____

_____

_____

_____

_____

STOP and Think: Are you willing to change some of your habits related to using social media?

_____

_____

_____

_____

_____

_____

_____

_____

_____

_____

Let's begin by looking at the many positive aspects of social media and how students with ADHD can benefit from its use:

Social Connection: As we have discussed, many neurodivergent students struggle with social relationships. After repeated experiences with rejection and bullying, some students find comfort in the safety of chat rooms and social media communities where there is a level of anonymity and a lower risk of humiliation. For those children, teens, and young adults who struggle to navigate the social nuances among their peers, utilizing virtual worlds of gaming, movies, and other forms of entertainment provides a comfortable setting to test and flex their social skills. People in these groups experience improved mental health and wellbeing because of the ability to share their collective experiences with one another.

Bridging Distance: Even under the best of circumstances, students who thrive socially still benefit from this digital tool. When friends from summer camp want to get together but cannot physically meet in person, FaceTime, Snapchat, and other platforms provide them with an excellent alternative.

Shared Interests: Beyond the shared experience of struggle, ADHD students find peers with whom they have other interests in common. Book clubs, artistic expression, the outdoors, photography, writing, and improvisational comedy are but a handful of interests kids bond over through social media. People who share interests use it as a gathering space to exchange ideas, solve problems, explore different forms and expressions of art, or simply connect over a shared sense of humanity.

Discovery: With such a rich array of easily accessible posts, users are exposed to concepts, practices, and experiences they may never have discovered otherwise. Many of my students can hardly contain themselves when they tell me about a new recipe they discovered on Instagram. My college students make plans for their semester abroad and create itineraries for their free weekends based on towns and cities they never knew existed until they explored posts made by world travelers. One of my clients became an avid floral designer after she started following a social media influencer who gave demonstrations on a floral design platform. In fact, a few local venues have hired her to create their flower arrangements for their events! The possibilities are endless, thanks, in part, to the resources available on social media platforms.

Resource: You have probably turned to social media for advice or guidance before for multiple reasons. Social media can offer a safe way to get answers to burning questions. YouTube and other platforms offer helpful tutorials about everything from curricular content to how-to-fix-it projects around the house. And we all know there is nothing you can't find on Google. Whether it's a how-to video about a small electronic repair or troubleshooting a particular software glitch, these videos are incredibly helpful. Similarly, there are thousands of influencers who pour out their hearts and souls, sharing their personal trials and tribulations. These individuals who struggle with learning disabilities, health issues, or a neurodevelopmental disorder like ADHD bring hope to their followers by sharing their personal testimonials.

Given all the benefits of social media, it's hard to understand why it would have such a negative impact on the mental health of our children's developing brains.

STOP and Think: How have you benefited from social media?

_____

_____

_____

_____

_____

_____

_____

_____

_____

_____

_____

William Shakespeare once asked, "Can one desire too much of a good thing?" Like anything in life, it's frequently helpful to use moderation. Social media is no exception. In the US Surgeon General's report about the impact of social media, Dr. Vivek Murthy released a warning about the risks related to the use of this tool. His report centered specifically on its impact on the mental health of individuals across the lifespan, including students in elementary school through college. Here are some of the key points in this report:

Brain Development: According to the Surgeon General's report, adolescents between the ages of ten to nineteen years old experience "a highly sensitive period of brain development [during this stage of their lives].[12]" This is the time in their development when engagement

---

[12] Office of the Surgeon General (OSG), _Social Media and Youth Mental Health: The U.S. Surgeon General's Advisory_ [Internet] (Washington, DC: U.S.

in risk-taking behaviors reaches an all-time high—and when their well-being is subjected to the greatest shifts. It is also the point in their growth when early signs of depression and anxiety emerge.

Equally important is the fact that personal identity and a sense of one's self-worth take form. The adolescent brain becomes susceptible to peer pressure, opinions, and comparisons. With these conditions serving as a fragile foundation, it should not come as a surprise that the frequent use of social media may be tied to specific changes in the adolescent brain in an area called the amygdala—the part of the brain responsible for emotional learning and behavior—as well as the prefrontal cortex, which handles impulse control, emotional regulation, attention and adjusting social behavior. The latter is the area of the brain that is most affected by ADHD, so it makes sense that kids who have been diagnosed with ADHD are even more susceptible to the negative impacts of using social media.

Mental Health: Studies about the risks related to the use of social media are extremely telling. In one research experiment involving a significant number of children ages twelve to fifteen years old, scientists discovered that spending more than three hours per day on social media "doubled the risk of poor mental health outcomes."[13]

A separate study found that social media negatively impacted the mental health of adolescent girls, particularly those who had already faced mental health challenges before using social media.[14]

Department of Health and Human Services, 2023), https://www.ncbi.nlm.nih.gov/books/NBK594763/.
[13] Kathy Katella, "How Social Media Affects Your Teen's Mental Health: A Parent's Guide," *Yale Medicine*, June 17, 2024, accessed November 11, 2024, https://www.yalemedicine.org/news/social-media-teen-mental-health-a-parents-guide.
[14] Katella, "How Social Media Affects Your Teen's Mental Health."

Additionally, an experiment involving 11,000 fourteen-year-olds revealed that increased social media use was linked to poor sleep, online harassment, negative body image, low self-esteem, and heightened depressive symptoms. These effects were more pronounced in girls than in boys.[15]

Cyber Bullying, Addiction, and Predators: When allowed to go unchecked and used improperly, social media is a fertile ground of real and present danger to unsuspecting young users. Cyber bullying is just as painful as the bullying that takes place in the hallways and the playgrounds. The anonymity of this means of virtual abuse makes it easy to post inappropriate content consisting of language and photo or video images. By their own admission, designers of social media apps created them in such a way that their platforms and algorithms are addictive and entice users to delve further and further into the virtual realm.

Worse yet, social media platforms are a feeding ground for predators who exhibit inappropriate behaviors—or, more concerning, some predators lure young users into engaging in sexually explicit activity or taking part in illegal activities, including the sale and distribution of drugs.

High School and College Students Are Just as Vulnerable: Younger children and adolescents are not the only demographics who are at risk of having problems related to social media use. Researchers introduced a specific social media platform to multiple colleges and found a direct link between its use and an increase in depression and

---

[15] Kate Kelland, "Social Media Linked to Higher Risk of Depression in Teen Girls," *World Economic Forum*, January 9, 2019, accessed November 11, 2024, https://www.weforum.org/stories/2019/01/social-media-linked-to-higher-risk-of-depression-in-teen-girls/.

anxiety among college-aged students.[16] If it can have such a powerful impact on the mental health of college students whose brains are more developed, imagine the effects it could have on children and adolescents, who are at an even more vulnerable stage of brain development. In my own practice, I have noticed the toll social media takes on my clients *and* their families:

Intrusion: Family meals are dotted with bleeps, bells, and bloops, enticing youngsters to respond to a text, Instagram post, or Facebook message. No one can complete a thought, and conversations are frequently left hanging. More importantly, it leaves people feeling like there's always something more important than the very individuals they're sharing the room with.

Sleep: Sleep patterns can be all but destroyed when phones remain in kids' bedrooms after the lights are turned off for the night. The screen's blue back light suppresses the production of melatonin, the hormone responsible for triggering sleep. When this happens, sleep is harder to come by. Users flit from one link to the next, and suddenly, it's 3 AM, and our poor night owl only has three hours remaining until he needs to get up for school. That wake-up call is going to be a beast!

FOMO: The fear of missing out is a genuine concern for many social media consumers. What are the group's weekend plans? Who is fighting with whom? Did they break up, or did they decide to stay together? Whose house is being toilet-papered tonight? Who won the latest round of Senior Assassin? When is my Fantasy Draft taking

---

[16] Dylan Walsh, "Study: Social Media Use Linked to Decline in Mental Health," *MIT Sloan School of Management*, September 14, 2022, https://mitsloan.mit.edu/ideas-made-to-matter/study-social-media-use-linked-to-decline-mental-health

place, and where? The questions are endless, and the curiosity that surrounds every answer is insatiable. But there is a very real price that comes with the fear of being left out, and *that* is anxiety. I have spoken with a lot of kids who become so overwhelmed at the prospect of not being 'in the know,' that they become unable to focus on their schoolwork—and unwilling to spend time with their friends and family. At some point, social media becomes an addiction.

Pressure: The pressure adolescents and teens feel to 'keep up' with their peers is very powerful and frequently hard to look past. These vulnerable users do not understand that the content shared on their peers' social media posts frequently presents an image of perfection or an ideal scenario, but the reality is that not every day is perfect; at some point, we all face challenges. However, hard times aren't exciting and frequently cause the users angst, so by posting an overly exaggerated positive version of themselves, they give others—and themselves—a false sense of reality that life is grand and couldn't be better.

The result? Viewers have a misguided notion of the quality of life they should aspire toward. They become convinced that failing to meet that standard means their lives are less noteworthy. The implications of this misguided mindset can be devastating—and sometimes fatal.

These consequences of social media use are just a few examples of the challenges that come with this internet-based form of entertainment and communication. For the neurodivergent population, social media presents specific difficulties, some of which exacerbate symptoms they already struggle with—even without social media use. The negative effects for students with ADHD can be just as significant, if not more so.

Time Blindness: One of the biggest challenges for those with ADHD is time blindness. The inability to perceive and track time is incredibly frustrating for this population. Ten minutes feels the same as two hours; consequently, estimating how long a particular task or assignment will take is challenging. The elusive nature of time makes planning one's day difficult.

When social media is thrown into the mix, all bets are off. Students tell me they take breaks from their homework and hop onto a social media platform, intending to scroll through posts for "just five minutes." However, given the enticing nature of the content, one swipe leads to another; one "like" leads to a comment, which leads to a reply, which sparks a question, and the poor kid is falling down the rabbit hole of Instagram posts. Two hours later, she's left wondering where the time went, and she's torn between staying up late to finish the overdue project or getting the rest she desperately needs.

Boredom: The rush we get when we participate in exciting activities can be addictive. This stimulation can extend to social media, including Instagram reels, Twitter feeds, videos, etc. With the flood of visual enticements pouring across our screens, impulse control can go out the window. Considering that, on an average day in the world of ADHD, controlling one's behavior is already difficult enough without help from social media. Adding an easily accessible activity can open the floodgates of excitement, sending even the most relaxed mind into stimulation overdrive. That adrenaline rush is very pleasing and can most certainly become too enticing to resist.

Social Interactions: It is not unusual for people with ADHD to struggle socially; often, their active and "noisy" minds prevent them from picking up on social cues. Their impulsivity is a turnoff to others. Social media provides a safe way to interact with others, particularly if the chat rooms are a gathering place for people who share similar struggles or interests. Suddenly, this kid has an eager audience, ready to listen to what they have to say. As we've discussed, finding one's voice and having a supportive group of listeners can be incredibly empowering. But not to rain on anyone's parade—it's easy to get swept up in the feel-good community of social media. That's why it's essential to have some guidelines to ensure the people in this virtual circle are who they claim to be. More on this in the suggestions section of this chapter.

Endurance/Higher Threshold for Frustration: The very nature of social media is instantaneous gratification. Think about it: You get immediate answers to your questions when you search Google. Shopping has never been easier, especially when you use Amazon—no sooner do you place an order than it arrives the next day, and you can do this all within the confines of your bedroom as you sit and stream shows on your tv or computer. While these features are certainly convenient, they have lowered our tolerance for frustration and compromised our endurance.

Kids with ADHD already come to the table with a lower threshold for frustration. It makes sense, right? Focus is frequently elusive, and consequently, so too is the stick-with-it-ness needed for problem-solving and time-consuming obligations. Grit and determination aren't qualities that come naturally to this neurodivergent population. Tasks that take concerted effort and time become increasingly unbearable. The add-water-and-stir nature of social media chips away at qualities like patience and endurance, rendering the users impatient and frustrated. How do we build these muscles back up? Let's consider some ideas.

STOP and Think: Have you noticed any challenges or negative consequences related to your social media use?

_____

_____

_____

_____

_____

_____

_____

_____

_____

_____

STOP and Think: What are they, and how willing are you to change some of your habits?

_____

_____

_____

_____

_____

_____

_____

_____

_____

_____

_____

The mood in the room has shifted since we started to identify the challenges that come with social media. It's suddenly serious and somber. Fear not, my digital virtuoso, all is not lost! Suggestions are heading your way!

Think about this analogy. Many of you love your desserts, right? I know my weakness is homemade ice cream. Whenever I visit a town or city for the first time, one of the first things I like to do is go to a local ice creamery and sample their scoops of delicious frozen delights. But as we have established in this chapter, it's important to use some common sense and balance. As is true for most of us, I must watch how much ice cream I consume to avoid an upset belly, right? And when I get home, I need to be sure to brush my teeth to get rid of the sugary residue that coats my choppers.

I'm not saying you need to avoid social media altogether. On the contrary, it's an integral part of the social world we all live in, especially for kids. I am merely suggesting you use good judgment when you pick up that phone or turn on your laptop. Here are some suggestions for your consideration.

General Guidelines for Family

Work with your family to establish device-free zones in the home, including the dinner table and bedrooms. It's better to not include phones during family mealtimes. Also, when it's time to go to sleep, it's better for phones to remain outside the bedroom. You and your parents should identify time parameters or duration of use.

Interestingly, in research that studied the impact of reduced use on mental health, psychologists found that reducing the time spent on social media improved mental health for both young adults and adults. Limiting use to thirty minutes per day over three weeks resulted in significant improvement in depression.[17] A separate study found that deactivating social media accounts for one month resulted in "improved subjective well-being," including satisfaction with life, happiness, and a decrease in anxiety and depression.[18]

---

[17] Jeremy Nobel, MD, MPH, "Is a Steady Diet of Social Media Unhealthy?" *Harvard Health Blog*, December 21, 2018, https://www.health.harvard.edu/blog/is-a-steady-diet-of-social-media-unhealthy-2018122115600

[18] Hunt Allcott, Luca Braghieri, Sarah Eichmeyer, and Matthew Gentzkow, "The Welfare Effects of Social Media," *American Economic Review* 110, no. 3 (2020): 629–76, https://doi.org/10.1257/aer.20190658.

Suggestion for Time Blindness

It's beneficial to avoid social media altogether during times designated for work. These platforms are addictive and irresistible by nature. Why tempt yourself to get pulled off track? Outsmart yourself! If you need a break when you're working, first, designate a set period to do so and decide ahead of time what that break will consist of. On My TOAD App™, the 3 2B-Me tool uses a three-part reminder system to snap the user to attention and return to work. Set timers to remind you to exit your platform of choice. Utilize software that blocks certain platforms—or literally cuts you off from your connection after a while. Use applications like the Down Time feature on your iPhone.

Here are some other ideas:

- Take a walk or go for a run.
- Walk the dog—your parents will definitely approve of that idea!
- Get a snack and a drink of water.
- Read the newspaper—the actual hard-copy version, not the digital one. (Nice try!)
- Talk with a friend on a landline—you know, the phone that's hanging on your wall in your kitchen, assuming your family still has a landline. If not, don't use your phone to call someone, as this could lead to checking your social media.
- Clean your room.
- Bake something.
- Set the table—another task that will meet with parent/guardian approval!
- Create something—draw, paint, throw pottery on the pottery wheel, build a model of something, build some parts of a computer, or write a poem or short story.

155

- Get a part-time job. Not only will this distract you from using your phone, but it may provide the opportunity for you to develop some important social and life skills. Plus, you will earn money as you go!

Suggestions for Boredom

You are clearly resourceful if you have navigated social media platforms and found people to follow who pique your curiosity, right? So, use these well-established skills to explore equally exciting and novel activities to investigate in the actual world.

- Hike around a lake.
- Learn about fly-fishing and master this art.
- Research locations and events that are popular in your hometown and experience them to find out why so many people like them (and yes, you can use the internet).
- If you are an artist or a music aficionado, find some local fairs and check out the artists.
- Go sample the goods at a local farmer's market.
- Train for an athletic event—marathon, half marathon—walk, bike, skate. Invite your friends to join you—the more the merrier!

Suggestions for Social Interaction

Only engage with people you know. Do not share personal information with anyone unless you know them. NEVER UNDER ANY CIRCUMSTANCES agree to meet anyone in person you do not know, and certainly do not meet with someone alone (even if you know that person)—bring a friend or adult with you.

Never ever share explicit photos of yourself with anyone online, even people you know. You cannot trust that this content will stay with your intended audience, even if they are a friend or a significant other. Relationships fray; people get angry with each other, and poor decisions are made. When these circumstances happen, there's no limit as to what can happen with that suggestive photo you shared with others.

Do not accept invitations to participate in inappropriate challenges, even if it is coming from someone you know. There is never a time when putting yourself or others in a compromised position or danger is okay.

Be respectful with the language you use and the posts you make. Don't post anything you wouldn't show your grandmother—or, more importantly, what you would not want to be posted about you.

Remember, your social media posts are like squishing toothpaste from the tube. Once it's out, you can put it back in, so you don't want to post something you'll regret the next day. The posts you put out on the internet can take on a life of their own and remain visible for a long time. Make sure that what you post is really what you want everyone to see.

IMPORTANT NOTE

For those of you who are considering applying to colleges, you may be interested to know that colleges look at your social presence. There have been instances in which an offer of admission has been revoked because the colleges did not like what they saw on an admittee's social media platform. Some schools have dedicated staff whose only responsibility is to search applicants' social media platforms; they take it *that* seriously. Don't make a mistake that will haunt you for four years.

Practice In-Person Interactions

- Order food at a restaurant.
- Get groceries at the grocery store.
- Go for a walk in your neighborhood.
- Work out in the gym.
- Hang out at the park.
- Make small talk with your postal service person when they deliver your mail.
- Help your neighbor.
- Invite a friend over to hang out.

Engage in Activities that Require Patience:

- Prepare a meal for yourself, family, or friends.
- Build something (birdhouse, model car—tech-savvy kids can build a computer).
- Put a small puzzle together—start with twenty-five pieces and move up to 50, 150, 250, 500.
- Take a walk and set a goal of saying hello to three people you encounter.
- Sit in your backyard or a park for fifteen minutes and notice everything taking place around you using your five senses.

Use timers to mark time as you work on these activities: start with a shorter chunk of time, maybe five to ten minutes, then add five-minute integrals as you build your endurance.

STOP and Think: Do any of these strategies resonate with you? Which ones are you willing to experiment with?

_____

_____

_____

_____

_____

_____

_____

_____

_____

_____

I fully acknowledge that social media is a powerful tool that offers an endless number of benefits to its users. If you just look at the first decades of the twenty-first century, we have witnessed this technology's global impact on more than one occasion.

The Arab Spring was a direct product of social media. Were it not for users' posts that cast a light on the atrocities that were happening in Tunisia, Libya, Yemen, Syria, Egypt, and Bahrain, the rest of the world may never have known the horrors taking place in these countries. Similarly, Volodymyr Zelensky and Ukraine most certainly would have fallen to Russia were it not for the widespread campaign this fearless leader launched over multiple social platforms.

Other movements like mental health, global warming, reproductive rights, gun reform, and school violence have all benefitted from this amazing means of connectivity and communication.

On a smaller scale, this population loves the social and entertainment benefits that come from social media. Whether it's a

FaceTime group call or an endless stream of texts between friends, this form of digital technology has been a lifeline for millions of users around the world. The opportunity to interact with like-minded individuals who share the same passions and interests is enticing and frequently serves to validate one's personal experiences. For children, teens, and young adults, living in this complicated, ever-evolving landscape called life, it helps to know others share and understand their day-to-day challenges.

If we are going to be honest, my insightful, tech-savvy reader, some challenges come with social media. Everyone's experience is different. I'll admit some students have creatively mastered the use of social media in such a way that it rarely impedes their ability to do work or interact with others in person.

However, in my years of working with clients who share your learning profile, more often than not, social media poses many challenges, including an increase in distractibility, poor time management, and the inability to complete work. Additionally, some of you may know friends or peers who have experienced increased levels of anxiety and depression directly related to their use of social media. The bottom line is that social media is a powerful form of digital technology, and it needs to be used responsibly.

Fear not! I am not suggesting you relinquish your phones and revert to using fax machines to communicate. That thought never even occurred to me. I am a realist. This technology is not going anywhere, and if anything, the science will continue to become more sophisticated. I won't be surprised if we start to welcome anagrams into our home, much like Obi-Wan Kenobi would communicate with Luke Skywalker. I am merely suggesting the importance of striking a balance that will allow you to enjoy the benefits while safeguarding your physical, emotional, and academic well-being.

What does this look like? Take a minute to reflect on the suggestions section of this chapter. Of all the strategies offered here, which ones do you feel are most appropriate for you? Which options could you see yourself trying and implementing into your daily routine? Can you envision a world in which you continue to use social media, but can implement and respect the boundaries you set for yourself?

Perhaps it would be helpful to enlist the help of your parents. I know, I know! You want as much autonomy on this topic as possible, and you still can, even if you involve your parents. Try this: you set the parameters.

You can find the pdfs for this material on my website: www.mytoadapp.com/chapter7.

Draw up a plan of action similar to this one:

Strategy	Accountability	Possible Obstacles	Solutions
Establish device-free zones	Make a list of places you agree not to use the phone: workspace, dinner table, bathroom.	Forgetting	Post a bright sticky note in that location to remind you to leave the device out of these spaces.
Silence notifications	Disable sounds and banners and batch them so they come all at once, only a few times per day.	Your curiosity may get the best of you.	Try it for one week and see if you notice a positive impact.
Create distance	Leave the phone in another room, especially when you are working, place it facedown so you can see the notifications, and put it behind a shelf or under a pillow so it is out of sight and mind.	Fear of missing out	Try these strategies a few times per day, starting with five-minute intervals and then slowly increasing the time.

Establish times of day when you do not use your phone	Meals, studying, family time, showering, right before bed	Forgetting	Set reminders in your phone. Leave phones outside of the room in which these activities are taking place.
Become the family ambassador of healthy device usage	Work with your family members to create family guidelines for devices	Not everyone will agree or follow the suggested guidelines	Set up an awards system; create partnerships between family members to hold each other accountable and to support one another.

You can take charge of your social media and device use. It may be challenging, but by taking small steps to find balance, you can create healthy change and navigate social media with more control, maximizing its benefits while minimizing its negative effects.

Key Takeaways: Chapter 7

✓ **Social media can be both beneficial and harmful** for students with ADHD, offering social connections and risks to mental health.

✓ **Guidelines and boundaries should be established** with parents or guardians to find a healthy balance with social media usage. You can play a critical role in deciding these parameters.

✓ **Using strategies to create device-free zones** in the home and setting time limits for social media can facilitate the prioritization of mental well-being and academic success.

✓ **Take precautions when engaging with others** on social media, such as only interacting with known individuals, avoiding sharing personal information, and being mindful of the language and content you use in your posts. Remember, once you post, it's out there for everyone to see.

✓ **Build endurance and focus by engaging in real-world activities**, exploring new interests, and using timers to increase attention span.

Conclusion:
Let's Bring It Home

You may wonder why I wrote this book. I have worked with thousands of students over the past twenty-five years, and while they all have struggled with ADHD and executive functioning skills, they each have a unique story.

Some of my clients have come to me defeated. After repeatedly encountering failure in numerous classes, year after year, they no longer believe they have the potential to succeed in school. Other students are filled with humiliation. They know they are smart; in fact, some of the most intelligent students I've ever met have ADHD. But they just can't get out of their own way long enough to establish and maintain any semblance of routine, preventing them from gaining traction on the path to academic and personal success.

For some students, the toll of walking hand-in-hand with ADHD has triggered mounting levels of anxiety. Homework, exams, and other high-intensity tasks frequently lead to panic attacks and, in some extreme cases, the avoidance of school altogether. The level of desperation and discouragement is significant and cannot be overlooked.

Finding Resilience

On the other hand, after significant struggle, many of my ADHDers have become quite resilient. They have established creative routines and protocols to keep them on task. They've found useful apps to track daily and long-term assignments, extracurricular activities, and appointments outside of school. Everything is recorded in one central calendar, with reminders sent via texts and emails across multiple devices. (And anyone reading this paragraph knows that the temptation to ignore a reminder is powerful, so having multiple reminders on multiple devices is going to be overkill or extremely helpful. Either way, you won't forget to do what needs to be done!) One of the best features of these apps is the accountability feature that allows you to mark a task as 'started,' 'in progress,' or 'complete.' As I mentioned earlier in the book, My TOAD App™ is chock full of tools that can help you with everything from time management to organization, accountability, and distractibility.

With a strong sense of self, they utilize their free time to participate in activities that reflect their passions: school plays, improvisational comedy, sports, instrumental music, vocal performances, technology and computers, politics, social causes... the list goes on and on.

There is no stopping these individuals, and many report to me that the self-esteem and sense of self-efficacy they reap from these pursuits empower them to face their academic challenges. Using that same self-awareness to help them identify the academic issues at hand, they work to identify strategies to address them. If there is nothing else, I want you to take away six important things from this book.

Number 1- You Are Resilient. You have had to be resilient to make it to this point in your academic career. Whether you're just starting your journey in elementary school, broadening your horizons in middle school, or strutting your stuff in high school or college, you're still in school and meeting with some success—none of which happened by accident. Along the way, you figured out how to do the school thing; maybe it hasn't been perfect, but clearly, you have some tricks in your bag.

Number 2- You Are Savvy. Oh my gosh, my clients are incredibly gifted problem solvers. While others, including adults, may spin their wheels, wedded to the idea of doing a particular task in a certain way, my students are adaptable and able to pivot when circumstances change.

I had a student who struggled mightily to complete schoolwork at home. With three younger siblings, two dogs, and a parent who worked from home, the ability to focus on homework was elusive. We discussed working in the attic or the basement, but neither of these options provided a space far enough away from the banter of the family's home. This student decided it was probably best to find a venue outside of the home, and find it, he did! On his quest to discover the "just-right place," he joked that he understood how Goldilocks felt on her mission to find the perfect chair, bed, and bowl of porridge. After experimenting at numerous locations, he settled on the local library; there was a bay window that overlooked the pond behind the building, and this peaceful setting was the perfect place to do his work. Victory!

Not so fast. Two months after spring break, the township initiated a renovation project at the park behind the library. Trees were trimmed back; bulldozers shifted massive piles of dirt from one side of the property to the other; and worst of all, the concrete trail needed to be replaced, which required the use of an army of jackhammers. Paradise was lost, but only temporarily.

My client had the forethought to bring his noise-canceling headphones to the library, and that did the trick. Though the room vibrated amidst all the turmoil outside, it was not enough to disturb this kid's concentration. He improved his grades in all but one class using this spot in the library. It was just right. So, what am I telling you? You have savvy in you. Get creative. Jump outside of that box, and search for the strategies and answers that work for you!

Number 3- You Are Not Alone. I would bet that if you polled your classmates, you'd learn that at least one-quarter of them struggle with executive functioning skills—*because* they have ADHD or because these skills just don't come easily to them. Managing time, organizing backpacks and personal spaces, completing and submitting homework, practicing self-advocacy, and developing study and test-taking skills are all challenges that many students find difficult to master and maintain. Those heated debates and battles you're having with your parents at home are playing out in houses throughout your neighborhood and across the country. Some kids speak openly about their struggles.

During a group meeting I hosted before COVID-19, one of my students found humor in a particular evening's shenanigans, a night she referred to as "The Great Homework Debate." While the details aren't important, the fact that she openly shared this event with me and her peers allowed everyone in the group to bond. So many of the students could relate as she shared bits and pieces of the dialogue from that night. Shouts of "Oh my gosh, that's the same thing my dad said to me the other night" or "We do that in our house, too" were refreshing for everyone to hear. They bonded over this shared mix of frustration about the circular conversations they often encountered.

While some students speak openly about their trials and tribulations with ADHD and its impact on their academic and personal lives, a significant percentage of students play it close to the vest.

Their sense of shame and embarrassment is too much to acknowledge, let alone share. Every morning, they don their masks of courage, trying to convince themselves and others that everything is okay, when the truth of the matter is that often putting one foot in front of the other is an accomplishment in and of itself.

Some of these students worry their secret life of academic struggle, late-night homework sessions, and procrastination booby traps will be exposed, thrusting their vulnerabilities into the spotlight. They don't realize how much they have in common with so many of their peers who struggle with the same challenges. There is tremendous pressure to maintain an appearance of having it all together because, after all, isn't that the truth?

Do we all have it put together? Not really. We all carry some kind of baggage with us daily. The size of the "bag" depends on the day and the issues at hand. Some days only warrant a receptacle the size of a large wallet, which is very convenient and easy to carry. Other days are so packed with emotion and difficulty that a full set of luggage is warranted. Some days are harder than others, but I will say the silver lining here is the harder the day, the more there is to be gained.

You learn how to manage the load, whether that means leaning on others or adjusting your goals so they are in alignment with what you can achieve in that moment. You master the art of pivoting and problem-solving so that when you find yourself in a similar situation, you can effectively navigate your way to the other side. You are not unique in this regard, which means you are not alone in your struggle, and I hope knowing that others share your experience will become a source of comfort to you.

Number 4- You Have Agency. You may have ADHD, but like I tell my clients, ADHD does not need to *have* you. While it may not feel this way sometimes, you have a lot of say in what happens in your life. "Woah, hold on a minute, sister. Say what?" you ask. Do you have a say in whether you have homework each night? Well, in some cases, you do. If you are allotted time in class to complete it and you choose to capitalize on that opportunity, then yes, the likelihood is you won't have homework that night.

At the very least, you may likely have a reduced workload. But in general, the assignment of homework is usually not in a student's control. However, you have a say in how, when, and where you do your homework. Consider these questions:

- ✓ Will you complete it on your own or work with friends?
- ✓ What time will you start? What time will you end?
- ✓ When do you want to complete your work?
- ✓ Where do you want to work? Will your place of operation be at a library, in your room, at the kitchen or dining room table, outside, at a coffeehouse, or bookstore?
- ✓ Will you play music or an app with ambient noise, or will you work in silence?
- ✓ Are you keeping snacks and a bottle of water by your side?
- ✓ When and how will you take breaks?
- ✓ What homework will you complete first, second, third, etc?
- ✓ How much time will you spend on each assignment?

When you look at homework this way, you may see that you have a lot more control over the situation than you think you do. You are the boss on every single one of these points. Choose what works best for you and run with it! And therein lies one of the main points of this book. I want this book to be a source of empowerment, an opportunity for you to supercharge your ADHD and your self-awareness so you can build your self-esteem and belief in your ability to succeed.

The ADHD brain is a challenging organ, and sometimes it's a brutally frustrating place to be, but if you can take the time to understand your neurodivergence and how your ADHD impacts your life, you can identify some strategies and skills that will help you become an independent and successful person.

Number 5-You Can Have Hope. Just as there are people out there struggling to navigate life with ADHD, there are just as many who have learned to succeed.

I worked with a girl who struggled to keep track of her assignments. She would either forget that she had deadlines to meet, or she would complete the assignment and lose it or forget to hand it in. Hours of hard labor were lost to the black hole of "I don't know where I put my homework." I would receive no fewer than three calls each week from her mother, who, with the best of intentions, tried mightily to help her daughter establish a system of homework that would provide some semblance of organization and personal accountability.

By the time the mother and daughter reached my office one night, they were both depleted, ready to put each other up on Craigslist. Little by little, we chipped away at the issues related to her productivity. She frequently felt overwhelmed at the prospect of initiating her homework each night. When she thought about starting her homework, all she could envision was an endless stream of tasks and late-night hours. She shut down before she could even begin her work. Further exacerbating the situation was the fact that she frequently left her materials at school, which meant she spent at least an extra hour trying to get the worksheets and links from her friends so she could just start her homework.

As we identified the obstacles that kept her from succeeding, my client realized things didn't have to be so hard. With a fresh perspective, she worked with me to establish strategies to help her work smarter and not harder. We also created some tips and strategies her mom could use to support her without undermining her independence.

This was not an overnight success story—it took time and patience on everyone's part before the ball started to roll and stay rolling in the right direction, but she did it. Eight years later, she is now a parent advisor, helping moms and dads understand the nuances of their neurodivergent students' learning profiles.

Number 6- Not Every Student is Open to Working with a Coach. For many students, getting help is an admission of weakness, as we discussed earlier in this book. They hitch their rope to the belief that with time and perseverance, they'll figure it out, and in some cases, this happens. I make it a policy not to work with this type of student. Most times, when the student doesn't want coaching services, it becomes an exercise in futility for the student, the coach, and the parents. The kid is already frustrated with himself and his struggle to succeed. These emotions get exacerbated when he's forced to do something he has deemed unhelpful.

But for one prospect, I was intrigued, and I took him on because something about him indicated, despite his overt resistance to my services, that a part of him was open to the prospect of meeting with success.

Admittedly, the first session wasn't an easy one for either of us. First, I posed some get-to-know-you questions: What were his interests? How did he feel about the Eagles's new quarterback? (Hey, he was an avid Philadelphia sports fan, and we shared a love of the Eagles, so I had to take his temperature!) We continued this banter for a few more minutes, and then I got serious, asking him how he felt about meeting with me.

"Pissed," he said with a straight face. I asked him to elaborate. "I'm pissed because my parents don't listen to me. I don't want to be here; it's not going to help. I can figure this out on my own. It's not like I'm failing out of middle school. I just haven't figured it out yet. It's all good. I got it."

As he spoke, a tear rose to the surface of his lower eyelid, and he quickly wiped it away, checking to see if I had seen his body's betrayal of his emotions. I made like I had seen nothing, and I continued to talk with him. When I asked him what his personal definition of success was, he looked at me as if I had slapped him across the face. His eyes grew large, and his mouth literally dropped open. "No one has ever asked me about any of this—until now," he said.

We kept conversing, and the more we chatted, the more his walls came crumbling down. He felt unheard: none of the adults in his life ever asked him how he felt about what was happening or what he thought might be helpful. He felt as though he was chasing after a standard of success his parents, teachers, and community had imposed upon him.

There was little consideration for his learning profile and what he could accomplish. The more he was offered "help," the more he grew frustrated and resentful. But things changed that year. Not only did he have a space to speak openly about his desires, goals, and hopes, but he could work to identify obstacles that would prevent him from succeeding and pinpoint strategies he'd need to overcome them.

He finally felt validated in his experience, and this affirmation was enough to give him the hope that one day, he could amount to something, even if it meant his path was less conventional than his peers. With this validation in place, he finally felt motivated to take the steps needed for success. Together, he and I coached his parents on his learning profile, working with them to find ways to encourage his independence while offering effective support that wouldn't undermine his efforts.

Hope is a powerful mindset that fuels so many of us in our quest to succeed. My hope for you is that this book has ignited at least a small spark of ambition from which you can build a large, glowing bonfire of self-discovery and empowerment.

Closing Thoughts

I believe in you and your ability to find your path to reach, if not exceed, your potential. There is too much evidence to think otherwise. You are here, and you have taken the time to invest in yourself and your self-worth by reading part, if not all, of this book. Take a minute to think about all you've accomplished up to this point in your life.

Think about your relationships. While they may not be perfect (no relationship is), you have established and maintained some of them. There is at least one class in which you are meeting with success. I don't care if it's your Auto Mechanic 101 or your AP US History class; you are passing the class—and by "passing," I don't necessarily mean you are earning an "A." You probably have interests you have pursued. You have asked teachers or friends for help in your classes.

Most importantly, you keep showing up. Regardless of the bumps and bruises, the humiliation and frustration, you keep putting yourself back in the game, ready to give it another shot, demonstrating your fortitude, resilience, and determination.

We all have the capacity for change, and you are no exception. There is no one right way to go about taking this journey; the only right way is the one that's right for you. So, get up and go stand in front of your mirror.

You can find the pdfs for this material on my website: www.mytoadapp.com/conclusion.

Assume a Superhero Pose

Make a fist in each of your hands.

Place each hand at the top of each hip.

Stand with your feet, hips-length apart.

Stand tall and puff out your chest as if you are a Superhero.

Look at yourself in the mirror, take a deep breath, and repeat after me. "I am capable. I am brave. I am resilient."

You *are* your own superhero. Now is the time to supercharge your ADHD and tap into your superhero powers. Your voice matters. Let it be heard. Advocate for yourself. Utilize the resources you have at your disposal, be it teachers, coaches, parents, or friends. Help them help you. Mistakes will be made; use them to your advantage and capitalize on the lessons learned so the "next time" is better.

In a world that may try to label and limit you, remember that your ADHD does *not* define you. Believe in yourself and your ability to reach your potential. Let those superpowers come through as you chart your own flight toward perseverance, self-awareness, resilience, and triumph.

I hope this book is helpful and provides tools you can use to reach your goals. Thank you for allowing me to be a part of your journey.

Take Action!

You made it! You read the whole book, and now you are wondering, "What's next?" Check out my executive functioning app, My TOAD App™.

I created My TOAD App™ to coach users about time management, organization, accountability, and distractibility. My TOAD App™ is the only comprehensive executive functioning app of its kind to offer this combination of effective tools needed to master skills related to these executive functions. Research has shown that proficiency in awareness and management of time, organizational skills, personal accountability, and the limitation of distractions are critical for countering struggles related to executive functioning. Our process begins with a straightforward onboarding process that results in a personalized plan of attack. Depending on the results of that process, the user has access to several tools:

My TOAD App™ begins with the opportunity for the user to ground themselves using the **Brain Dump** tool. The **Time Management** feature offers a **Master Calendar** to plan out and schedule works and school-related tasks, and the **Task Estimator** facilitates the awareness of time.

The **Organization** feature offers the **Task Manager** tool where users can organize their work, school, and life projects and tasks, and the **How-To** tool provides AI-informed guidance to simplify common tasks related to work, home, and school. **Workspace** gives users the opportunity to develop their ideas related to any given task-whether it's a research project, a pitch to the boss, or organizing a dinner party, this is a great space to externalize ideas. The **Get to Do List** is a helpful tool to track what needs to get done on any given day. For those users who tend to lose personal belongings, the **Lost and Found** tool helps the user decrease the number of items they misplace as well as the frequency with which they lose them while simultaneously identifying effective places to store these belongings and assisting in the location of items that have been misplaced. This helpful information is stored in the app, so users can reference it the next time they need to locate their belongings!

The **Accountability** feature offers the **3 2B-Me** tool that reminds users to begin their tasks. Additionally, the **SOS** tool enables the user to reach out to others to aid in the process of accountability. **Accountability Tabs** help the user to keep track of which tasks have been initiated, those that are in progress and completed, and those that require additional assistance.

Finally, the **Distractibility** feature hosts the **Ambient Noise** tool which offers a fun array of ambient sounds and music to choose from to quiet external and internal noise.

My TOAD App™ is intended to be used as a supplement to or independent of life or academic coaching.

Check out My TOAD App™:

Acknowledgments

I could not have embarked on this journey without the support of my husband, Mark, and my two sons, Evan and Zach. Your encouragement is often what fueled me to the finish line. Bu, you have always been my strongest champion. Your patience and steadfast support never wavered, even when my work pulled me away from our morning walks, our meals together, and nightly television shows. Evan and Zach, your enthusiasm, creativity, and patience with my technological shortcomings meant more than I can express. Collectively, the three of you have been my sounding board, my problem-solvers, and my biggest cheerleaders. From the moment I first announced, "I'm going to write this book," you believed in me and the mission behind it—to validate and support those who need it most. I couldn't have done this without your love, patience, and belief in both me and this cause.

I would not have the amazing final product that is hero-worthy were it not for the support and enthusiasm of my readers. Penny Moldofsky, Craig Coleman, Janet Snellenburg-Kline, Anna Mallory, and Robin Bass, your thorough read of my manuscript and eye for detail resulted in a rich and user-friendly finished product. I valued the time and energy you devoted to helping me create a resource I am extremely proud to present to the world.

To Madeleine Weiser, lovingly called "Dr. Maddy", who has not only cared for my children with kindness and dedication over the past 22 years but has also been a true partner in my journey to support the neurodivergent community, I extend heartfelt gratitude. Your trust in my work, from referring families to my practice early on in my career to taking the time to review my manuscript, has played a meaningful role in helping me build something that truly makes a difference. I am deeply grateful for your generosity, insight, and steadfast support.

Thank you to Dale Michaels who introduced me to the world of ADHD. He suspected that this demographic and my passion for helping others were a perfect fit, and I proved him right. Our study sessions led to mastery of content, and the strategies he taught me (many of which have informed those found in my book and my app) have become the basis of my secret sauce in my own practice. I am grateful for his guidance and mentorship.

Kim Coghlan, I don't think either of us wanted to edit one more iteration of this manuscript! Thank you for your support as I navigated writing my first book. Your partnership made the process seamless and painless and frequently boosted my confidence when I was feeling that vulnerability that comes with being a first-time writer. Thank you for your guidance that went well beyond the bounds of editor, including marketing strategies (even those that included social media!), proposal letters, and the determination of an appropriate publishing route. I can't wait to partner with you again.

I am very grateful to Annika Winkelmann for her incredible talent in transforming my words into vivid, exact illustrations that perfectly capture the message of this book. Her patience, dedication, and willingness to collaborate made this journey so enjoyable, and I couldn't have asked for a better creative partner.

Jodi Lyons, thank goodness for Brandeis University! I am so grateful for your guidance and friendship over the course of the past two years. You were the first established author to roll out the red carpet, welcoming me into the world of authorship. Our first conversations gave me the confidence I needed to get this ball rolling. Thank you for your accessibility and willingness to act as a mentor, sounding board, and friend.

I am so grateful to the incredible team of coaches (past and present) I have worked with at AcademicAlly, LLC. Your creativity, problem-solving skills, and expertise in ADHD not only inspire our clients but also equip their families with the tools and understanding they need to support their children's growth and success.

So much of what we do as coaches—empowering students with self-awareness, practical, transformative strategies, helping them build confidence, and guiding families toward a better understanding of ADHD—is reflected in the pages of my book. While the book was my own writing journey, I couldn't have done it without the inspiration I draw from working alongside such a dedicated and talented team. Your commitment to this work, and the impact you make every day, embodies the very principles and tools shared in these pages: meeting students where they are, helping them discover their strengths, and giving them the skills to thrive.

Thank you for your passion, your expertise, and the difference you make in the lives of the students and families we serve. I am grateful to be on this journey with all of you.

To my many colleagues-there are too many of you to name- who have joined me in the trenches, you will never know how much I have appreciated and valued your collaboration on behalf of our shared clients and patients. It is an honor to share the ADHD journey with each of you. I have learned so much from the conversations we have had, and I look forward to continuing to serve the neurodivergent population and their families with you in the years to come.

Mom and Dad, thank you for teaching me the power of independence and for supporting and encouraging me on this incredible journey. Your example of working with and helping others reach their potential has shown me the importance of passion, advocacy, and making a meaningful difference in the lives of those around me.

Emby and Fil, thank you for your steady support and encouragement as my dream became a reality. Your belief in me means more than you know, and I am so grateful for both of you.

Finally, to the thousands of clients and their families I have had the privilege of working with, thank you for allowing me to co-pilot your flight to growth and independence. You are amazing, and you have so much to offer the world. I often catch myself in a coaching session wondering who is learning more, you or me. Were it not for you, this book would never have been written. I believe in you and your *superpower*.

About the Author

Hannah Bookbinder, LSW, M.Ed. has worked with the neurodivergent population for over 25 years. With a bachelor's degree in psychology from Brandeis University, a master's in social service from Bryn Mawr College, and a master's in elementary education from Cabrini University, she established AcademicAlly, LLC to assist individuals struggling with executive functioning skills. Over 95% of her clients have a formal ADHD diagnosis, and she works with individuals ranging from second graders to adults.

Hannah's experience has given her a deep understanding of the challenges faced by those with ADHD and their families. Time management, organization, accountability, distractibility, and self-advocacy are just a few of the hurdles these clients face daily. She has seen firsthand the frustration, misunderstandings, and relational strain that can arise—and she is dedicated to helping families navigate these challenges with clinically proven strategies.

In collaboration with psychiatrists, psychologists, educators, and neuropsychologists, Hannah has developed effective tools to empower her clients. She has also shared her expertise through articles, blog posts, and presentations, offering actionable strategies to parents and professionals.

As a member of organizations such as NASW and CHADD, she stays up to date on the latest ADHD research. Her website, www.Academic-Ally.com, provides additional resources, including her blog, *Here's the Thing*. Hannah's executive functioning app, My TOAD App™, will be available in the spring of 2025. This app is being developed for individuals across the lifespan who struggle with executive function skills like time management, organization, accountability, and distractibility. Information about this app can be found using our QR code in the "Take Action!" section of the book or at www.mytoadapp.com.

Hannah is passionate about helping clients reclaim control over their lives, and she often reminds them: "You may have ADHD, but ADHD does not need to have you." Her book and app are designed to provide comprehensive tools that empower neurodivergent individuals to succeed.

When she's not writing or coaching, Hannah can be found lacing up her sneakers for a long walk (preferably with her husband or good friends) or enjoying a night of television with her family. She loves finding homemade ice cream shops when traveling, fashion, and walking along the beach. Hannah shares her life with her husband, Mark, their two sons, Evan and Zach, and their beloved fur baby, Rocky—who may or may not think he runs the household.

Bibliography

ADDitude. "ADHD and Hyperfocus: The Fascinating Connection."
    Accessed October 14, 2024.
    https://www.additudemag.com/adhd-symptoms-hyperfocus-
    attention/.

Allcott, Hunt, Luca Braghieri, Sarah Eichmeyer, and Matthew
    Gentzkow. "The Welfare Effects of Social Media." American
    Economic Review 110, no. 3 (2020): 629–76.
    https://doi.org/10.1257/aer.20190658.

Centers for Disease Control and Prevention. "Data and Statistics About
    ADHD." CDC. Last reviewed September 20, 2022.
    https://www.cdc.gov/adhd/data.

CHADD. "General Prevalence." CHADD: The National Resource on
    ADHD. Accessed September 23, 2024.
    https://chadd.org/about-adhd/general-prevalence/.

CHADD. "Overview of ADHD." CHADD: The National Resource on
    ADHD. Accessed September 23, 2024.
    https://chadd.org/about-adhd/overview/.

Forbes. "ADHD Statistics." Accessed September 23, 2024.
    https://www.forbes.com/health/mind/adhd-statistics.

Katella, Kathy. "How Social Media Affects Your Teen's Mental Health: A
    Parent's Guide." Yale Medicine, June 17, 2024. Accessed
    November 11, 2024.
    https://www.yalemedicine.org/news/social-media-teen-
    mental-health-a-parents-guide.

Kelland, Kate. "Social Media Linked to Higher Risk of Depression in Teen Girls." *World Economic Forum*, January 9, 2019. Accessed November 11, 2024. https://www.weforum.org/stories/2019/01/social-media-linked-to-higher-risk-of-depression-in-teen-girls/.

Kohn, Michael R., Leanne S. Clarke, and Vaughan J. Casey. "Assessing the Efficacy of a School-Based Intervention Program for Adolescents with ADHD." *ADHD Attention Deficit and Hyperactivity Disorders* 2, no. 1 (2010): 41–48. https://doi.org/10.1007/s12402-010-0045-8.

Nobel, Jeremy, MD, MPH. "Is a Steady Diet of Social Media Unhealthy?" Harvard Health Blog, December 21, 2018. https://www.health.harvard.edu/blog/is-a-steady-diet-of-social-media-unhealthy-2018122115600.

Office of the Surgeon General (OSG). *Social Media and Youth Mental Health: The US Surgeon General's Advisory* [Internet]. Washington, DC: US Department of Health and Human Services, 2023. https://www.ncbi.nlm.nih.gov/books/NBK594763/.

Tardiff, Sara. "Simone Biles Called Dropping Out of the Tokyo Olympics Her 'Biggest Win.'" Teen Vogue. April 14, 2022. https://www.teenvogue.com/story/simone-biles-called-dropping-out-of-the-tokyo-olympics-her-biggest-win.

US Department of Health and Human Services. "Surgeon General Issues New Advisory About Effects Social Media Use Has on Youth Mental Health." May 23, 2023. https://www.hhs.gov/about/news/2023/05/23/surgeon-general-issues-new-advisory-about-effects-social-media-use-has-youth-mental-health.html.

Walsh, Dylan. "Study: Social Media Use Linked to Decline in Mental Health." MIT Sloan School of Management, September 14, 2022. https://mitsloan.mit.edu/ideas-made-to-matter/study-social-media-use-linked-to-decline-mental-health.

Wilens, Timothy E., M.D "ADHD and Substance Abuse: The Link & How Stimulant Medication Can Help." ADDitude. Accessed October 16, 2024. https://www.additudemag.com/adhd-and-substance-abuse-stimulant-medication/.

Wilens, Timothy E., M.D. "Treating a Child with ADHD Medication Diminishes His Future Risk of Substance Abuse." *ADDitude*. Last modified May 22, 2024. From the webinar "ADHD and Substance Use Disorders: How to Recognize and Manage Addiction in Adults and Adolescents." https://www.additudemag.com/adhd-and-substance-abuse-stimulant-medication/.

Yoga With Adriene. *Yoga With Adriene*. (YouTube channel). Accessed October 16, 2024. https://www.youtube.com/yogawithadriene.

Resources

Here are some additional resources you may find helpful:

Apps

- **Headspace.** This app utilizes mindfulness and meditation to empower users to reduce their stress, improve sleep, and increase resilience. Through tools like guided meditation, sleep casts, mindful movement, focus exercises, and daily inspirations, Headspace provides a user-friendly pathway to manage stress and anxiety.
- **Insight Timer.** This app provides users access to free and paid meditations and yoga exercises any time of day or night. There are over 220,000 guided meditations for every level of experience.
- **My TOAD App™.** The purpose of the MY TOAD App™ is to assist individuals who struggle with executive functioning skills like time management, organization, accountability, and distractibility. Users will become more independent and successful at managing their daily academic, professional, and personal responsibilities. TOAD creates a customized plan of attack for each user utilizing a variety of tools related to time management, organization, accountability, and distractibility. To learn more, scan our QR code in the "Take Action!" section of this book.

Books

- **ADHD 2.0** by Edward Hallowell and John Ratey. The authors describe ADHD's biological causes and its most prominent symptoms. They discuss ways to minimize ADHD's downsides and maximize its benefits, such as finding the right kind of challenge to stay engaged and building a strong support network. Our commentary will provide further insight into what causes ADHD as well as what it's like to live with the condition.

- **Driven to Distraction (Revised): Recognizing and Coping With Attention Deficit Disorder** by Edward Hallowell and John Ratey. Groundbreaking and comprehensive, this book has been a lifeline to the approximately eighteen million Americans who are thought to have ADHD. The authors explore the varied forms ADHD takes, from hyperactivity to daydreaming. They dispel common myths, offer helpful coping tools, and give a thorough accounting of all treatment options as well as tips for dealing with a diagnosed child, partner, or family member. But most importantly, they focus on the positives that can come with this "disorder"—including high energy, intuitiveness, creativity, and enthusiasm. Now the bestselling book is revised and updated with current medical information for a new generation searching for answers.

- **Late Lost and Unprepared: A Parent's Guide to Helping Children With Executive Functioning** by Joyce Cooper-Kahn and Laurie Dietzel. This book is dedicated to helping parents understand ADHD and help their children establish EF skills.

- **Nowhere to Hide: Why Kids With ADHD and LD Hate School and What We Can Do About It** by Jerome J. Schultz and Edward Hallowell. The author addresses the consequences of stress related to learning disorders and ADHD and the destructive repercussions of the stress on students' academic, social, and emotional well-being. The book aims to inform parents about their children's experiences while providing practical strategies that have been proven stress reducers in and out of the classroom.

Magazine

- **Attention Magazine.** CHADD's bimonthly magazine provides information to individuals who have ADHD, their families, and educators.

Websites

- **CHADD (Children and Adults who have ADHD).** www.chadd.org. A website that provides resources, information, and support to children and adults who have ADHD and their families.
- **NIMH National Institute of Mental Health.** www.nimh.nih.gov. This government agency offers information about ADHD, including statistics, symptoms, and diagnosis.
- **CDC (Center for Disease Control).** www.cdc.gov. The CDC provides basic information about ADHD, including symptoms, diagnosis, and treatments.
- **COPAA (The Council of Parent Attorneys and Advocates).** www.childmind.org. Helps parents secure educational services for children with disabilities. Tools and strategies to help manage time, stay focused, and handle homework.

YouTube

- **Yoga With Adriene.** www.Yogawithadriene.com. Yoga instructor Adrienne Mishler offers yoga instruction to viewers of all levels. Her humor and grace shine through with every session.
- **Mindful Walking Meditation with Jim Brickman.** www.jimbrickman.com. This fifteen-minute mindfulness

meditation is a unique way to incorporate being present into any walk you take. The three grounding exercises he uses are extremely tangible and effective for the most difficult minds to tame.

Organizer

- **Out of Chaos Planner.** This unique pen-paper planner allows students to see their assignments alongside their school and weekend activities. Everything is located in one location. Students only have to enter their classes (up to seven spots are available) once instead of having to re-write their classes each week. Available on Amazon or other websites.